T0365655

Get on Board and Stay on Board is a delightful and down-to-earth collection of wisdom for life by Pearl Kumi. This volume contains many short 1-2 page essays and poems that could be read with great profit by anyone seeking to understand and know God better. The pages are full of quotations from the Bible which informs the worldview of the author. The author writes clearly, concisely, and centered on Christ. Whether a reader professes to be a follower of Jesus or not, this volume will help them understand why Paul wrote, "for to me to live is Christ" (Philippians 1:21). The brevity of the articles and frequent changes of subject make *Get on Board and Stay on Board* a good choice for a daily devotional resource.

> Dr. George Harton
> President, Washington Bible College

My life has been enriched by Pearl Kumi. She introduced my wife and me to peanut soup. But even better she gives us the 'milk' and the 'meat' of the Word of God - the Bible - through her poems and devotionals. You will be strengthened in faith as you read the words contained here.

> Wayne D. Lawton,
> Pastor Cedar Hill Community Church,
> Elizabethtown, Pennsylvania

GET ON BOARD AND STAY ON BOARD

Jesus Is Calling/Saved, Now What/Special Days

Pearl Nsiah-Kumi

WestBow
PRESS
A DIVISION OF THOMAS NELSON

ISBN: 978-1-4497-6178-3 (sc)
ISBN: 978-1-4497-6179-0 (e)

Library of Congress Control Number: 2012914100

WestBow Press books may be ordered through booksellers or by contacting:

WestBow Press
A Division of Thomas Nelson
1663 Liberty Drive
Bloomington, IN 47403
www.westbowpress.com
1-(866) 928-1240

Because of the dynamic nature of the Internet, any web addresses or
links contained in this book may have changed since publication and
may no longer be valid. The views expressed in this work are solely those
of the author and do not necessarily reflect the views of the publisher,
and the publisher hereby disclaims any responsibility for them.

Any people depicted in stock imagery provided by Thinkstock are models,
and such images are being used for illustrative purposes only.

Certain stock imagery © Thinkstock.

Printed in the United States of America

WestBow Press rev. date: 9/12/2012

DEDICATION

To my grandchildren: Kaylee, Aiden, and Blaine;
with a prayer that they will come to faith in Jesus
at a young age and live for Him.

TABLE OF CONTENTS

Section Three: Special Days

SECTION ONE:
JESUS IS CALLING

GOD

Most people worship a deity they call God, and some like to believe it is the same God everybody worships, regardless of how. I say it's not the same God. How can I tell?

+ My God is a triune God, consisting of the Father, the Son and the Holy Spirit. "Then God said, 'Let us make man in our image, in our likeness." Gen 1:26

    "For in Christ all the fullness of the Deity lives in bodily form." Col 2:9

    If you can't say this of your God, then you have a different one.

+ My God became flesh and dwelt among men, in the person of Jesus Christ. "The word became flesh and made his dwelling among us. We have seen His glory, the glory of the One and Only, who came from the Father, full of grace and truth." Jn 1:14

    Is this true of your God?

+ My God hates sin, loves the sinner, and so made provision for sin by dying in the person of Jesus Christ. Jn 3:16 Is this true of your God?

+ My God died in the person of Jesus and was buried, but did not see decay. He rose again on the third day. Acts 2:31-32 Is this true of your God?

- My God ascended into heaven forty days after his resurrection. Acts 1:3b, 9-11 C

Can you say that about your God?

- My God is offering salvation to all who will believe in Jesus, because He said of Him, "This is my Son, whom I love; with Him I am well pleased. **Listen to Him**." Mt 17:5b The Son, Jesus said, **"I am the way and the truth and the life. No one comes to the Father except through me." Jn 14:6**

If your God is not offering salvation, he definitely is not the God I know.

- My God is coming back to earth in the near future, and every eye shall see Him. Acts 1:11 Is yours coming back?

- My God promises life after death. "For the wages of sin is death, but the gift of God is eternal life in Christ Jesus our Lord." Rom 6:23 How about yours?

If any of these truths are not true of your God, then we are not worshiping the same God. That makes me very concerned about you, because there is only one God. You might just be trying to do the best you can, and hoping that in the end, it would turn out that you've been worshiping the One and only true God. That is a dangerous position to take. Don't wait to die to discover that the God you worshiped did not really exist. If your intentions are to worship the One and only God, the Creator of the universe, then the only way to Him is through Jesus Christ. Trying to get to God any other way will not get you there. Why? Because the Bible says, "God our Savior wants all men to be saved and to come to the knowledge of the truth. **For there is one God and one Mediator between God and men, the Man Christ Jesus, who gave Himself as a ransom for all men."** 1 Tim 2:4-6a I understand that you might be finding it difficult to admit you've been wrong and you've been misled, but it is better to be wrong now than later. Admit it now, and come to God through Jesus Christ. Put your faith in Jesus, today! He will save you and give you the assurance of salvation to put your mind to rest. "I write these things to you who believe in the name of the Son of God (Jesus) so that you may know that you have eternal life." 1 Jn 5:13

Don't let pride stop you!

IT IS PERSONAL

"Religion is a very personal matter," you say
You do not appreciate people asking you what you believe
"Religion is a very personal matter," you say
You don't want to talk about it
What is so personal about it?

"Religion is a very personal matter," you say
You think everybody should deal with it in their own way
"Religion is a very personal matter," you say
You don't want to discuss it
What is wrong with a little discussion?

"Religion is a very personal matter," you say
You think it is the same God we all worship, so "why the fuss"
In reference to Jesus Christ, God says, "this is my beloved Son hear Him."
Jesus Christ says, "He who believes in me has eternal life"
Won't refusing Christ indicate you have a different God?

"Religion is a very personal matter," you say
And rightly so since no one can believe on your behalf
"Religion is a very personal matter," you say
And rightly so, since no one can repent on your behalf
Seeing it's so personal, shouldn't you talk about it now?

Religion is a very personal matter,
You need to personally repent,
Ask God for forgiveness through Christ
He will wash away your sins and make you a new creature

Religion is a very personal matter
In the end, you will stand before God on your own behalf
So you are right, religion is a very PERSONAL matter
It is also URGENT, talk about it today.

KNOWING CHRIST IN A PERSONAL WAY

None righteous

"For all have sinned and fall short of the glory of God." Rom 3:23

"For the wages of sin is death, but the gift of God is eternal life in Christ Jesus." Rom 3:23

Christ is the only way to God (for salvation and everyday living)

"I am the way and the truth and the life. No one comes to the Father <u>except</u> through me." Jn 14 : 6

"For there is one God and <u>one mediator between God and men</u>, the man Christ Jesus, who gave Himself as a ransom for all men." 1 Tim. 2: 5

"If you confess with your mouth, "Jesus is Lord", and believe in your heart that God raised Him from the dead, you will be saved. For it is with your heart that you believe and are justified, and it is with your mouth that you confess and are saved." Rom 10:9-10

Assurance of Salvation

"I write these things to <u>you who believe in the name of the Son of God</u> so that you <u>may know</u> that you have eternal life." 1 Jn 5 :13

"Therefore, there is now no condemnation for those who are in Christ Jesus, because through Christ Jesus the law of the spirit of life set me free from the law of sin and death." Rom 8:1-2

DEATH IS NOT THE END

Many people today strongly believe death ends it all. Hence they don't really care how they live. They have the mentality of, "Let's eat and drink for tomorrow we die." 1 Cor 15:32b This mentality is not only wrong; it is far from the truth; it is a lie from the devil, the father of lies. He has an agenda. That agenda is to get as many people as possible to hell; after all why should he go there alone? He knows unbelievers are hell-bound. "Then he will say to those on His left, 'Depart from me, you who are cursed, into the eternal fire prepared for the devil and his angels.'" Mt 25:41 So his goal is to deceive and draw many to hell with him.

The truth about everything, including life after death is how it's defined by the Bible. Until we discover God's truth about issues we have no truth at all. So let's see what the Bible says about the subject of life after death. The Bible says, ". . . man is destined to die once, and after that to face judgment." Heb 9:27 This is how it's going to happen, "When the Son of Man (Jesus) comes in His glory, and all His angels with Him, He will sit on His throne in heavenly glory. All the nations will be gathered before Him, and He will separate the people one from another as a shepherd separates the sheep from the goats." Mt 25:31-32 Right there, we see there will be only two groups; there will only be believers and unbelievers. There will not be an in-between group. So when this separation is made, where will you be? The believers get to inherit the kingdom of God and the unbelievers get to inherit hell. Mt 25:34, 41

The book of Revelation talks about another kind of death. It is referred to as the second death. Rev 20:6 If there will be a second death, then natural death (1st death) does not end it all. There will be a second death which is referred to as the lake of fire. "Then death and Hades were thrown into the lake of fire. **The lake of fire is the second death.**" Rev 20:14 The Lake of fire will be ongoing, it will never go out or go down in its intensity, and it will be forever. Each person needs to make plans for life after the natural death. Whether one believes there is life after death or not does not change what God says about it, and God will not change His word because somebody does or does not believe it. If there's ever going to be a change of mind about any of God's laws, it is definitely not going to be God's. Each person can plan to go to heaven or face the second death. Each person has been given the right to make a choice. **God will not be responsible for anyone going to hell, those who go will do so by choice.** He said to the Israelites, "This day I call heaven and earth as witness against you that I have set before you life and death, blessings and curses. Now choose life, so that you and your children may live." Deut 30:19 He also says, "For the wages (payment) of sin is death (the 2nd death), but the gift of God is eternal life in Christ Jesus our Lord." Rom 6:23" For God so loved the world that He sent His only begotten Son that whosoever believes in Him should not perish but have everlasting life." Jn 3:16

The way God separates the sheep from the goats is to see whose name is or isn't written in the book of life. "If anyone's name is not written in the book of life, he was thrown into the lake of fire (2nd death)." Rev 20:15 Getting one's name in the book of life is understanding and admitting that one is a sinner, and cannot save himself or herself. Believing in Jesus, asking Him for forgiveness, and surrendering to His Lordship ensures that one has passed from death to life. What are you going to choose?

ETERNITY

Quite often when people die, you hear their loved ones say, "he or she is in a better place." This is a comforting thought, and I am sure everybody will like to think that about their deceased loved one. Before we go any further, we need to ask ourselves, "Where is this better place, and how do people get there?"

The Bible talks about eternity, either in heaven or in hell. There are no neutral places, so when people talk about a better place they most likely are referring to heaven. However, heaven is not an automatic destination for the deceased. When people die, their loved ones can comfort themselves any way they want, but that does not guarantee their loved one is in heaven. The biblical truth is, only those who believe on the name of Jesus will go to heaven; only those whose names are written in the Lamb's book of life.

People who do not believe on the name of Jesus Christ before they die cannot be wished or prayed into heaven by loved ones, not even by the church.

Eligibility into heaven is not based on gender, age, social or political standing. It is also not based on good works or anything else people do. It is based solely on the sacrifice Christ made on the cross, making Himself a bridge between God and man. Christ died to pay the penalty for sin, making the way for sinners to come to God by faith in Him (Jesus).

This is your opportunity. Ask Jesus to forgive your sins now. He will forgive you, take away the guilt of your sins, fill you with His Spirit and give you peace and the assurance of salvation. He will also write your name in His book of life. Don't count on your loved ones or your priests to wish or pray you into heaven after your death. It just does not work that way.

If you refuse Christ's offer for salvation, you have automatically and personally decided to go to hell after you die. Remember nothing can be changed about that decision once you are on the other side of dirt. So while you are on this side of dirt make the decision that guarantees you will spend eternity in heaven. Your loved ones can then say confidently, at your passing, "he or she is in a better place." Please make this decision soon, hopefully today.

MERCY SEAT VS JUDGMENT SEAT, PART I

The seats refer to the two separate encounters man is going to have with God, now and later. Each person has the option to appear at one or both seats. It is important to note that the seats are available at different times, under different circumstances and for different reasons. Going to the Mercy Seat (MS) is strictly by choice, and is for one reason only, **to obtain mercy.** Going to the judgment Seat (JS), will be for one of two reasons. For the Christian, it will be to give an account of himself to God, and to receive a reward. Rom 14:12 For the unbeliever, it will be to hear the verdict for not accepting God's offer of salvation. "No one can see the kingdom of God unless he is born again." Jn 3:3 It matters, very much, which seat one goes to first.

The Mercy Seat is available to all, for as long as they have life, and as long as they are capable of making decisions. The invitation to the Mercy Seat is simple; it became available with the death of Christ, "For God so loved the world that He gave His one and only Son that, whoever believes in Him shall not perish but have eternal life." Jn 3:16 At the MS, there is forgiveness, cleansing, new life now, and eternal life in the life to come. At the MS, all who want may come!

The JS comes after this life, and is not so much by choice. It is the way God has set things up. For those who never appeared at the Mercy Seat, the JS is by default. They have indirectly and gladly made a choice to accept without complaints, the verdict that is pronounced at the JS. They've missed the opportunity to receive pardon. There will be no second chances there, sorry. "Man is destined to die once, and after that to face judgment, so Christ was sacrificed once to take away the sins of many people; and He will appear a second time, not to bear sin, but to bring salvation to those who are waiting for Him." Heb 9:27-28 As misused as the word is, hell is really a place. It was prepared for the devil and his angels, but "If anyone's name was not found written in the book of life, he was thrown into the lake of fire." Rev 20:15

The book of Matthew puts it this way, "When the Son of man comes in His glory, and all His angels with Him . . . all the nations will be gathered before Him, and He will separate the people one from another as a shepherd separates the sheep from the goats . . . . then the King will say to those on His right, 'Come, you who are blessed by my Father; take your inheritance, the kingdom prepared for you since the creation of the world.' . . . Then He will say to those on His left, 'Depart from me, you who are cursed, into the eternal fire prepared for the devil and his angels.'" 25:31-41

God is not interested in anyone going to hell, and that was the reason He sent His Son to pay the penalty for our sins. He wants people to stop in at the MS and be forgiven; the price for sin is already paid. Christ died for sins, once! He is not going to do that again. Of course He would, if it were necessary, but God is completely satisfied with the one sacrifice, for all time. Don't be expecting any other way by which to escape hell. The 'good works' (kind deeds) route won't work, because He has already said, "All our righteous acts are like filthy rags." Isa 64:6b and please don't say, "There isn't only one way to heaven.", because there is only one way to heaven. "I am the way and the truth and the life. No one comes to the Father except through me." Jn 14:6

Choose life while you still have the opportunity. Tomorrow might be too late. Disbelief won't help; turning up your nose at God won't either. In humility, please go to the MS, believe in Jesus, and find forgiveness and the assurance of eternal life. Refusing to go to the MS means, one has elected to gladly live with the pronouncement from the JS. Please go to the Mercy Seat, today. This could be your last call to believe in Jesus!

MERCY SEAT VS JUDGMENT SEAT, PART II

Appearing at the Judgment Seat is just like appearing at a ticket counter to pick up reserved tickets for a scheduled event. There will be no family or group reservations. Each individual has to make their own reservation, and pick up their own ticket.

Remember that each one makes a reservation to where they want to go. The tickets usher people to one of two places. There are no in-between destinations. So where are people headed? One group is headed to claim their inheritance, the kingdom prepared for them since the creation of the world. Mt 25:34. The second group is headed to hell, a place prepared for the devil and his angels. Mt 25:41b

The ticket to the first destination remains good and ready for pick up at the right time with one piece of identification, the blood of Christ. "When I see the blood I will pass over you." Ex 12:13 "Since we have now been justified by His blood, how much more shall we be saved from God's wrath through Him." Rom 5:9

The ticket to the second destination is good only on the day of pick up; in other words, it can be cancelled before maturity. "Let the wicked forsake his way and the evil man his thoughts. Let him turn to the Lord, and He will have mercy on him, and to our God, for He will freely pardon." Isa 55:7

The practice in hospitals these days is to have patients and or their families sign all kinds of consents on admission. One of the consents is about resuscitation. Patients are allowed to turn down interventions that will keep them alive or prolong their lives. Belonging in the second group means the same thing. People are signing their own death warrant. By not choosing life they are choosing death.

After giving the life of His Son, God has every right to use this declaration against the unyielding, "This day I call heaven and earth as witnesses against you that I have set before you life and death, blessings and curses. Now choose life, so that you and your children may live." Deut 30:19

How are you going to respond to God's loving call? Are you still digging in your hills? "Seek the Lord while He may be found; call on Him while he is near." Isa 55:6 Speaking before the Sanhedrin, Peter the Apostle said of Jesus, "Salvation is found in no one else, for there is no other name under heaven given to men by which we must be saved." Acts 4:12 Don't wait any longer! Believe in the name of Jesus and be saved.

MISERY LOVES COMPANY

Satan was a lead angel in heaven. He was beautiful, referred to as the morning star, son of the dawn! Isa 14:12a, but he rebelled against God when he said in his heart, "I will ascend to heaven; I will raise my throne above the stars of God; I will sit enthroned on the mount of assembly, on the utmost heights of the sacred mountain. I will ascend above the tops of the clouds; I will make myself like the Most High." Isa 14:13-14a What was the result of his pride, ambition, arrogance and rebellion? He was thrown out of heaven! "How you have fallen from heaven, O morning star, son of the dawn!" Isa 14:12a His doom was sealed. There was no hope of redemption for him. Ever!

Satan does not have the privilege that humans have; the privilege to be saved from sin and death, and he knows it. Hell was prepared for him, his demons and all those who will follow in his footsteps, through disobedience to God. Mt 25:41 Desiring to defy God and also make sure he will not be the only resident in hell, the devil embarked on a journey to lie and deceive men so they will disobey God, one way or the other. He uses different strategies with different people. He makes different sins appeal to different people and suggests to them why these sins are okay. He doesn't really care which sin is committed, just as long as it is committed. Any sin will do, because he knows sin is lawlessness. 1 Jn 3:4b

When we sin, we break God's law, and that constitutes disobedience, and nothing makes the devil happier. He considers God his competitor; so any time we disobey God; I think he goes to his imaginary scoreboard to mark it down, and to keep count of how many people obeyed him rather than God. He even dared to get Jesus to obey him rather than God. How sad! In Deuteronomy

6:16, God clearly commanded the Israelites "Do not test the Lord your God." But what did the devil do? He tempted Jesus to do exactly what God had forbidden. He wanted Jesus to jump off a cliff, to display His power as the Son of God, and to see if God would really charge His angels to ensure His safety. Mt 4:5-8 Jesus didn't even have to think about His response. Immediately, He quoted Scripture to silence the devil; "It is written 'Do not put the Lord your God to the test'." Mt 4:7

The devil's campaign to lure men to sin against God started in the Garden of Eden. He deceived Eve by sowing doubt in her mind about what God had said, "Did God **really** say, 'You must not eat from **any** tree in the garden'?" Gen 3:1a After Eve responded, he refuted by saying, "You will not surely die . . . you will be like God, knowing good and evil." Gen 3:4-5 As a result, Adam and Eve disobeyed God; hence sin entered the world, and has since then passed on from generation to generation. Cain killed Abel out of envy and jealousy. Sin had come to stay, but "Thanks be to God for His indescribable gift", Christ Jesus. 2 Cor 9:15

Satan made a number of attempts to foil the plan of salvation, but failed. He has not given up; he is still working, fiercely, to deceive as many as he can, to bring them to hell. He is working harder now than ever, knowing that his doom is near. Armed with the knowledge of his doom, he wants to ensure he will not be the only resident in hell. How does he hope to achieve his goal? He hopes to achieve his goal by using his old tricks of: lying, twisting the truth, misquoting Scripture, etc. to entice humans to sin against God.

He knows that, "The wages of sin is death, but the gift of God is eternal life in Christ Jesus our Lord." Rom 6:23. So he knows that succeeding in turning people against God translates into having lots of company in hell. He must be thinking, if he can't escape hell, he should at least take others with him. Mt 25:41 Like they say, "Misery loves company." It is sad to think the devil's hard work and intentions are going to succeed. His success is being made possible by those who have turned their backs on Jesus, thinking and saying there is nothing after death. They continue to use arguments like, "Jesus is not the only way", "I am not as bad as . . .", "I am a nice person etc. etc. When it comes to salvation, nothing can and nothing will alter God's plan; it is faith in Jesus plus nothing else!! Jesus' death will not be in vain. It will accomplish what it was planned to accomplish, and that is the salvation of people who repent, calling on Jesus for forgiveness.

The devil knows his future; whether he likes it or not, he cannot change it. He is on his way to hell for interfering with God's plans. People who have not repented are also on their way to hell, but they still have the opportunity to be saved if they will repent in this life, and believe in the name of Jesus. This is the only time they have and it is running out. Don't be company for the devil in hell; he has nothing good to offer, except weeping and gnashing of teeth. Mt 8:12

PROCRASTINATION

Are you a procrastinator? Webster defines procrastinate as: put off, delay, postpone, drag your feet, defer and dally. Many people have problems with procrastination, but they do eventually get around to taking care of business. Sometimes though, they don't, and miss important deadlines as a result.

Different people procrastinate about different things. Some missed deadlines are opportunities gone forever, and no amount of regret can change that. If you drag your feet about a bill, you might have to pay it later with interest and life will still go on.

However, there is one critical deadline that affects every individual, man or woman, young or old, and the Bible calls it the Day of Salvation. 2 Cor 6:2b

It is a critical deadline because the Bible also says, "Man is destined to die once, and after that to face judgment." Heb 9:27

The Day of Salvation is a critical deadline because if missed, (unsaved before death) the destination after judgment is hell, a place originally prepared for the devil and his angels.

So you might say, "Which day is the Day of Salvation?" It is different for each person, but it is the day a person is confronted with the gospel (good news) of Jesus Christ. So for you dear reader today is your day. Don't let the sun go down without you settling this issue. Below is the gospel in a nutshell:

1. You are a sinner (you have a sin nature) Rom 3:23
2. The payment for your sin is death (hell) Rom 6:23
3. Jesus is the Son of God, the only Savior appointed by God. "Salvation is found in no one else, for there is no other name under heaven given to men by which we must be saved." Acts 4:12

4. Jesus died in your place so you can be saved through Him. 1 Tim 2:6
5. What you need to do is:
   - Repent and believe in Jesus
   - Confess you sins to Him,
   - Ask for forgiveness and He will forgive you 1 Jn 1:9

You might have heard this before, but did nothing about it. Head knowledge about the gospel does not save you; you need to believe it by believing in the name of Jesus. By God's grace you have been given another opportunity. Please don't put it off any longer; you might not have this opportunity again. Make your decision today, because tomorrow could be too late. "Now is the time of God's favor, now is the Day of Salvation." 2 Cor 6:2b

THE GUARANTEED PASSWORD

Codes, Passwords and Personal identification numbers
They are meant to keep others out of our business
Do you have a bank account?
Don't forget your code
Else you can't get your money out in a hurry

Codes, Passwords and Personal identification numbers
They are meant to protect our privacy and prevent fraud
Do you have a credit account?
Don't forget your code
Else you can't get any account information over the phone

Codes, Passwords and Personal identification numbers
They are designed to protect our privacy
Do you have a telephone answering machine?
Don't forget your password
Else you can't check your phone messages

Codes, Passwords and Personal identification numbers
We each have so many different ones and have become so
dependent on them
How about the password to get into heaven? Do you have it? It is
the most important one
That password is, "I BELIEVE IN JESUS!"
It is not a secret,
It is guaranteed to unlock the heavenly door for all who desire to
enter
No one gets into heaven without it

To obtain that password, place your faith in Jesus; confess your sins to Him

Ask for His forgiveness; He will wash and cleanse you from all unrighteousness

He will turn your life around; set you on the path to peace and victory

Whereas the codes and passwords in our lives are secrets,

The password to heaven should be shared freely, always, and gladly

JESUS SAVES!! Pass it on.

THE ROAD MAP

A map is a great tool for getting to unfamiliar places
If you were trying to get from point A to point B
And had no idea how to get there,
Most likely, you will ask another who knew,
Or get a map and follow it closely

As long as you are in this world, you are on a journey, you are going
somewhere
It doesn't matter how long it takes, you will get there, eventually
But where are you going, and do you know how to get there?
I suggest to you, it will be one of two places, heaven or hell
You can't go to both, it has to be one or the other
Where you go is your choice

To get to heaven, the road map you need is the Bible
It is God's word, written by men inspired by the Holy Spirit
In it, you learn that you are a sinner, deserving to die
But you also learn that God's Son, Jesus Christ died in your
place
What you need to do then, is acknowledge your sins before God;
ask for forgiveness
Place your faith in His Son, Jesus
He will wash your sins away and send his Spirit to dwell within
you
He will help you through his Spirit and the Bible to travel this
life
And most assuredly, at the end, bring you safe into heaven
Where mansions have been prepared for you
And for ever you will be in his presence,

To get to hell, you just have to ignore the map that directs to heaven

Live as you please, have no regard for God, your creator and His Son Jesus Christ

And you will undoubtedly end up in hell

But why would you want to end up there?

It is a place of torment and sorrow, with weeping and gnashing of teeth

The torment never ends

You most likely don't want to go to hell, you'd rather go to heaven

But you are trusting your good works (the acts of kindness and the like) to take you there

The Bible says you are saved by grace, not by works lest any man should boast

Your good works are simply not good enough,

God has made only one provision for salvation, the blood of Jesus Christ

Choose the road map that leads to life eternal by believing in Jesus

On the other hand, you probably don't even know you are traveling

Let alone have a destination in mind

But as long as you are in this world, you are traveling

And will end up somewhere, sooner or later

Make sure you are following the right road map!

THE TIME IS NOW

Are you one of the many who think time is on their side? Such people postpone every decision they need to make pertaining to God and eternity. If you are, you probably say things like, "I am young," "I am too busy," "I am in good health" or "I'll do it later."

If you had full control of your circumstances, you could get away with procrastinating, and at just the right time of your choosing, you could decide to believe in Jesus and be saved, and everything would be fine. Unfortunately for you, you don't have much control of your life, you don't get to decide when and how you die; God does.

Maybe end of life issues don't cross your mind often because life at present is going so well for you. That's what happened in the days of Noah. The Bible says people were eating and drinking, marrying and giving in marriage until the flood came (an indication that life was going on as usual when the flood came). Mt 24:37-38 Of course, by the time the flood came, it was too late (Gen 6-7). Their end had come suddenly, when there wasn't much time for them to call on God.

No matter how enjoyable you find this life, be reminded that it is only temporary. The end will come when you least expect it. All that the world has to offer cannot pay for your salvation. Only the blood of Jesus is acceptable as payment for your sins. The Bible says, "What good will it be for a man if he gains the whole world, yet forfeits his soul? Or what can a man give in exchange for his soul?" Mt 16:26 Think about it.

Young people are being advised to start planning now for retirement; so they can live comfortably in their later years. By the same token, your soul will live forever; you need to make provision for that. Where would you like to spend eternity, in heaven or in hell? If you prefer heaven, you'll need to take the steps now to guarantee it. When the jailer in the book of Acts asked Paul and Silas, "Sirs, what must I do to be saved?" Acts 16:30, they replied, "Believe in the name of the Lord Jesus, and you will be saved." v 31

The way to salvation has not changed, and never will. God decided the blood of Jesus was what it was going to take for Him to forgive sins. So Jesus came and shed His blood. Now it is up to you to believe in Him, confess your sins, ask for forgiveness and accept salvation through His blood. On the other hand if you'd rather spend eternity in hell, ignore the invitation to believe in Jesus, and you will be guaranteed to go to hell. But why would you choose that? Jesus loves you; that is why He died such a painful death. Choose life today!

"Now is the time of God's favor, now is the day of salvation." 2 Cor 6:2

THROUGH GOD'S EYES

How do you see yourself?
You probably see yourself as a helpless, hell-bound sinner
How does God see you?
He sees you as a sinner with the potential for godliness.

How do you judge yourself?
You probably judge yourself as hopeless and fit for hell
How does God judge you?
He judges you as fit for hell, but redeemable

How do you see yourself?
You probably see yourself as fit for heaven based on your good deeds
How does God see you?
He sees you as unfit for heaven on account of your good deeds

Friend, see yourself through God's eyes
You are a sinner by nature, deserving hell
No amount of good deeds you do will save you
Instead, believe on the name of Jesus Christ and be saved!

TIGHT SECURITY

Why has air travel become so frustrating? Why do we have to be at the airport hours before departure time? Why do we have to remove our shoes, hats and so forth when going through airport security? And why can't we take drinks or food through security? The answer is simple. The government is trying to ensure that no individual with evil intentions (terrorists) is allowed on an airplane. In short, it is a way of securing our safety. I am sure the bad guys have not given up yet; they are still trying, and hoping that one of these days, they'd succeed.

Recently, at a White House Dinner Party, an uninvited couple was able to get through security, and mingle with guests. When questioned they made up stories like, they had forgotten to bring their invitation, etc. They posed for pictures with dignitaries, and had a good time. So apparently, tight security in places does not guarantee that the uninvited would be kept out. It is still possible for the uninvited to go through security without being stopped or identified as uninvited guests, regardless of their intentions, until it is too late.

There is one place though that a guest without the proper credentials cannot bypass security, unnoticed. Look at this verse with me, "If anyone's name was not found in the book of life, he was thrown into the lake of fire." Rev 20:15 No one can sneak into heaven! There's not going to be an issue of oversight, mix ups, or excuses. Either your name is, or is not in the book of life. This is a very crucial issue.

How does one get his or her name in the Book of life? No name will get there by chance, or by being God's favorite. God is not in the business of playing favoritism. Jesus said to his disciples, "For whoever does the will of my Father in heaven is my

27

brother, and sister and mother." Mt 12:50 Also, Jesus promised to acknowledge before the Father, those who acknowledge Him before men; likewise, to disown before the Father, those who disown Him before men. Mt 10:32-33

Names are placed in the Book of life intentionally, for one reason only. "I tell you the truth; whoever hears my word and believes Him who sent me has eternal life and will not be condemned; he has crossed over from death to life." Jn 5:24 So as you see, it is by God's grace through faith in Jesus Christ that one is saved. It is also important to note that the Book of life does not have names of groups. Hence no one can be written in the Book of life because they belong to a particular Church, family, school or denomination. Each one is on his or her own. Each one has to come to Christ as an individual. No one can wish himself/herself into heaven; no one can do enough good deeds to qualify getting into heaven.

This is the assurance the believer has that his/her name is in the Book of life, "Therefore, there is now no condemnation for those who are in Christ Jesus, because through Christ Jesus the law of the Spirit of life set me free from the law of sin and death." Rom 8:1-2 "I write these things to you who believe in the name of the Son of God so that you may know that you have eternal life." 1 Jn 5:13

Would you like to get into heaven? Did you say, "Yes"? How do you plan to get there? Are you hoping to sneak by security somehow? That will not work. The only thing that will work is repentance and faith in Jesus. Accept Jesus as your personal Savior today. Jesus Christ is the only Way! Guaranteed!

THE TOUR GUIDE

A tour guide shows the way to places
Places he is very familiar with
He knows the history, current events as well as potential future
ones
He guides with ease, excitement and confidence
He knows the areas to avoid as well as the popular attractions
The area he guides tourists to, is his territory
He can answer any questions posed to him regarding that place
He does not tire talking about his territory
He is eager for everyone to see it
If you ever want to know a place well, and enjoy your visit
Get a guide.

You are passing through this world
You have very limited time
In order to know and enjoy your stay, you need a guide
Someone who knows this place well
What better someone than the one who created it, and created
you
God is waiting for your call, through His Son Jesus Christ
He wants to be your guide
He will direct and instruct you as to how to live
And in the end, bring you safely home
He is excited about the things He wants to show you now
Like; faith in Him, living an abundant life,
Living peaceably with yourself and others
He is the Guide you need.

A tour guide is limited in his knowledge
He knows only his territory
Outside of his territory, he might be of no help.
Heaven and earth belong to God, He made them both
He has no limitations in knowledge
You can trust him completely, any day any time
Call on Him today and let Him be the guide you so desperately
need
Your time here is short, make the best of it
Get the Guide now.

WAIT NO LONGER

You forgot to set your alarm
Running late for work, you hurriedly got ready and rushed out
You forget your wallet at home, which means you, had no money
or ID
But you made it through the day somehow
The next day was better; you had everything you needed for
work
So you see; some forgotten things in life are retrievable

How about if you miss the opportunity to go to heaven?
Do you think you'll get another opportunity?
How do you suppose that will happen?
Here's the truth, once you die, you cannot change anything
No amount of prayers said on your behalf after your death will
Not even the beautiful eulogy read at your funeral will make a
difference

If you want to go to heaven, you have to plan for it now
This plan is more important than any you'll ever make
It's good to have a will and a living will
The executors of your will cannot determine your destination
You are the only person who can and should make that decision
For your will to be legal, you have to write it out
You have to say exactly what you want done after your death
You have to sign and date it in the presence of a witness

By the same token, you have to decide your destination, heaven
or hell

If it's heaven, repent, believe in Jesus and ask Him in prayer, to be your savior
The Holy Spirit will bear witness to your decision and give you that assurance
Your name will be written in the book of life
And whenever it comes time to go, you'll be ready
Make this decision now because you have no idea when you'll be taking your last breath
Wait no longer!

On the other hand, if you desire hell for your destination
Do nothing different, continue to live in sin and you'll be sure to get there
But why would you want that?
Please, choose life and choose it now! Wait no longer!

WHAT IS TRUTH

Truth is the real state of things
It does not change
Truth is the real state of things
You are free to believe it, whatever it is
It will not change
Truth is the real state of things
Feel free to doubt it, whatever it is
It will not change to accommodate your doubt
Truth is the real state of things
Feel free to ignore it, whatever it is
It will not change
Truth is the real state of things
Argue about it all you want
It will not change

The Bible is the word of God
It does not change
What it says about you is true, you are a sinner
Argue about it all you want
The fact will not change
The soul that sins, it shall die, but the gift of God is eternal life
Refuse to believe it, blaspheme it, shove it aside
You still will not be exempted from the consequences of unbelief
Heaven and Hell are real
The facts will not change
At the end, you will stand before a holy God to give an account
He will announce where you spend eternity
It is His right to do so
But you think God is too good to send anyone to hell

But God is also, too faithful to go back on His word
He does not change and He makes no apologies

Since you cannot change any of these facts
Be wise and accept Christ's offer for salvation
He is calling and waiting
He says, "Believe in the name of the Lord Jesus and you will be saved"
He will not wait forever, "Behold I come quickly."
That is the TRUTH.

IT IS HIS RIGHT

Heaven belongs to God
He decides who goes there
He also decides the terms

You might disagree with his decisions
But that will not change anything
You could even make suggestions to sway him
But that will not make any difference

Heaven belongs to God
He decided the only ones allowed there, are those whose sins are forgiven
He also decided the only way to forgiveness is through faith in His Son Jesus

You might disagree with His decisions
You probably think, regardless of what people believe
He created all so all should be allowed in
You probably also think, whoever you judge as good should be allowed

Heaven belongs to God and not to you,
He does not need your advice or suggestions
He can do with heaven as He pleases

Heaven belongs to God
He is not going to excuse your unbelief because you disagree with Him

How often do you allow others to dictate to you what you should do with your property?

Heaven belongs to God
If you desire to go there, you have to follow his direction
Confess with your mouth the Lord Jesus
And believe in your heart that God raised Him from the dead
And you will be saved.
There is no other way.

GOD LOVES YOU, REALLY

The Bible says God has no delight in the death of the sinner. "For I take no pleasure in the death of anyone, declares the Sovereign Lord. Repent and live!" Ezek 18:32

He proves that fact in at least four different ways.

- First, He sent his Son to pay the penalty for sin. "For God so loved the world that He gave His only begotten Son that whosoever believes in Him should not perish but have everlasting life." Jn 3:16

- Second, He put His word into writing, the Bible, and instructed Christians to take the message to the entire world, so that they may be saved. "Everyone who calls on the name of the Lord will be saved. How then, can they call on the one they have not believed in? And how can they believe in the One of whom they have not heard? And how can they hear without someone preaching to them? And how can they preach unless they are sent?" Rom 10:13-15a

- Thirdly, He has delayed His return to allow more time for people to get saved. "The Lord is not slow in keeping His promise, as some understand slowness. He is patient with you, not wanting anyone to perish, but everyone to come to repentance." 2 Pet 3:9

- And lastly, He is elated every time a sinner repents. "There is rejoicing in the presence of the angels of God over one sinner who repents." Lk 15:10b

The synonyms for 'rejoicing' include: Joy, elation, delight, satisfaction, jubilation and exultation. Will God, the Creator of the universe, be rejoicing? It must be a big deal when a sinner repents. I can just imagine the angels cheering as He; the Creator claps, and takes to the dance floor.

Justice is one of God's attributes, and that compels Him to judge sin. Loving us does not interfere with His nature. Parents sometimes say to their children who keep disobeying, "Don't make me." I believe in the same way, God really doesn't want to have to judge or punish us, but we leave Him no choice, when we refuse to respond to his love. His joy is in seeing sinners come to repentance not in seeing them die in their sins. If you have not believed in Jesus, the Son of God, for your salvation, don't wait any longer. Tomorrow is not promised to anyone. Repentance is not possible after death, so repent today, while you are able to, and call on Jesus to save you. Don't make Him send you to hell. Honestly, He doesn't want to, but He will if you "make" Him. He will not compromise His nature to accommodate your stubbornness and disbelief.

SECTION TWO:
SAVED, NOW WHAT?

FREEDOM

Webster defines freedom as: 1. having personal rights or liberty.
                                          2. Independent,
                                          3. without charge

To be free or to seek freedom, one would have had to first be in bondage prior to seeking freedom. When in bondage, one has no personal rights, and therefore cannot do as one pleases. That individual always has to answer to a master. Freedom from bondage always has a price tag, payable by the slave or a third party. Freedom is not free.

Although the one who is freed is without charge, the one who paid the price lost or gave up something of great value like, money, life, reputation, etc.

From the day man sinned in the garden, he became a slave to sin and the devil. The only acceptable atonement for sin is the blood of Christ. God loved us so much He sent Jesus, His only Son to pay the price for sin. He made freedom available to all who will believe in Him. So now we the redeemed don't have to follow the dictates of the devil. We have the right to live godly lives. We are free to choose right over wrong.

He freed us from:

The power of sin
"For sin shall not be your master, because you are not under the law, but under grace." Rom 6:14

The guilt of sin
"Let us draw near to God with a sincere heart in full assurance of faith, having our hearts sprinkled to cleanse us from a guilty conscience and having our bodies washed with pure water." Heb 10:22

The penalty of sin
"For the wages of sin is death, but the gift of God is eternal life in Christ Jesus our Lord." Rom 6:23

He freed us to:

Live righteously-
"No one who is born of God will continue to sin, because God's seed remains in him; he cannot go on sinning, because he has been born of God." 1 Jn 3:9

Choose righteously-
"But if serving the Lord seems undesirable to you, then choose for yourselves this day whom you will serve, ... But as for me and my household, we will serve the Lord." Jos 24:15

Walk in newness of life-
"I will give you a new heart and put a new spirit in you; I will remove from you your heart of stone and give you a heart of flesh. And I will put my Spirit in you and move you to follow my decrees and be careful to keep my laws." Eze 36:26-27; "Therefore, if anyone is in Christ, he is a new creation; the old has gone, the new has come." 2 Cor 5:17; "And to put on the new self, created to be like God in true righteousness and holiness." Eph 4:24

Willingly serve—
"Worship the Lord your God, and serve Him only." Mt 4:10

". . . to love the Lord your God, to walk in all His ways, to obey His commands, to hold fast to Him and to serve Him with all your heart and all your soul." Jos 22:5b

MEMORIZE—"So if the Son sets you free, you will be free indeed." Jn 8:36

THE ATTRIBUTES OF GOD

GOD IS:

Creator of the universe: "In the beginning God created the heavens and the earth." Gen 1:1

Spirit: "God is Spirit, and His worshipers must worship in spirit and in truth." Jn 4:24

King/Ruler:" For God is the King of all the earth; . . . God reigns over the nations." Ps 47:7-8

Great: "How great is God-beyond our understanding! The number of His years is past finding out." Job 36:26

God Alone: "For you are great and do marvelous deeds; you alone are God." Ps 86:10

". . . you alone are God over all the Kingdoms of the earth." Isa 37:16

"Turn to me and be saved, all you ends of the earth; for I am God, and there is none other." Isa 45:22

"I am God, and there is no other; I am God and there is none like me." Isa 46:9

Greater than man: "But I tell you, in this you are not right, for God is greater than man. "Job 33:12

Our Salvation: "Surely God is my salvation; I will trust and not be afraid." Isa 12:2

Mighty and Greatly to be Feared: "In the council of the holy ones God is greatly feared; He is more awesome than all who surround him. O Lord God Almighty, who is like you? You are mighty, O Lord, and your faithfulness surrounds you." Ps 89:7-8

Holy: "Exalt the Lord our God and worship at His holy mountain, for the Lord our God is holy." Ps 99:9 "Be ye holy for I am holy." Lev 20:7

Love: "Whoever does not love does not know God, because God is love." 1 Jn 4:8

Merciful/compassionate
"The Lord is gracious and righteous; our God is full of compassion." Ps 116:5

Light: ". . . God is light; in Him there is no darkness at all." 1 Jn 1:5

Faithful: "God, who has called you into fellowship with His Son Jesus Christ our Lord, is faithful." 1 Cor 1:9

". . . . For no matter how many promises God has made, they are "yes" in Christ. And so through Him the "Amen" is spoken by us to the glory of God." 2 Cor 1:18-20

"By myself I have sworn, my mouth has uttered in all integrity a word that will not be revoked." Isa 45:23

Provider: "And my God will meet all your needs according to His glorious riches in Christ Jesus." Php 4:19

Our God: "So do not fear, for I am with you; do not be dismayed, for I am your God." Isa 41:10

BE A SAINT

Who is a saint, and when does one become a saint? There are people who think sainthood is pronounced upon a person after their death, based on how good/holy they lived. According to the Scriptures, saint is another name for Christian. The apostle Paul addressing the Church at Ephesus called them saints; "Paul, an apostle of Christ Jesus by the will of God, to **the saints** in Ephesus, the faithful in Christ Jesus." Eph 1:1 These addressees were alive, so one does not need to be dead to be called a saint. Hence those of us who are in the body of Christ Jesus are saints, whether we are in or out of our individual earthly bodies.

Having established that we are saints, we should also establish that unless the Lord draws us we cannot come to Him (Jn 6:44), and therefore sainthood is a calling. Paul writing to the church in Rome addressed them this way, "To all in Rome who are loved by God and **called to be saints."** Rom 1:1 The online dictionary defines **Call** as: 1) Making a request or demand, 2) Speaking in a loud distinct voice so as to be heard at a distance, and one of the definitions for **to be:** is to become. So CALLED TO BE SAINTS means, God requested/demanded that we become saints. To become something different from what we are requires a transformation from one state of being to another (Example: going from a cocoon to a butterfly). We are transformed from a state of unbelief/ungodliness to belief/faith in Christ, resulting in the newness of life and the renewal of the mind. We are not called to act like saints; we are called to be saints.

Sainthood is not a cloak we put on and take off when we feel like it. We are to be saints around the clock, 24/7. It should be our new nature, our state of being. We are to be saints at home, away from home, when we are awake and when we are asleep. We should be saints at all times; in the company of believers as well as in the company of unbeliever, no matter what. 'Saint' should be our identity; the identity by which we are known.

How can we vibrantly maintain our sainthood? Let's compare sainthood to professions in the circular world. We need to have the mindset that we are saints. We need to learn all we can about being saints, by studying the manual for saints, by attending in-services, seminars, and training sessions about saints. This will equip us to get better at being saints. The word says we should not neglect the assembling together of the saints, as some are in the habit of doing, but we should encourage one another (Heb 10:25). It also says we should correctly handle the word of truth. 2 Tim :15b Every so often, professionals go through certification and re-certification to ensure their skills and knowledge are up to date. We receive our certifications and re-certifications through the trials we go through to confirm that we are applying the lessons we learn on how to maintain our sainthood.

Sainthood is ongoing, and takes perseverance. We should get better at being saints with the passage of time as we keep our gaze on Jesus, the author and perfecter of our faith. Heb 12:2a

EVIDENCE OF INTIMACY WITH JESUS

We all like others to know who our friends are; we sometimes prove that friendship by how much we know about each other. When people have been friends for a long time, they begin to think and act like each other. There is a saying I haven't heard in a long time that proves this point. It goes something like this, "Show me your friend and I'll show you your character."

In a similar way, Peter and John, by their courage, proved to the members of the Sanhedrin that they had been with Jesus. In Acts chapter four, Luke gives the account of how Peter and John responded when questioned by the Sanhedrin, "By what power or what name did you do this?" V 7b (Referring to the healing of a cripple).

Peter wasted no time; he went straight to the point, proving that Jesus was the Christ and that through Him, the cripple had been healed.

The Scripture tells us, "When they saw the courage of Peter and John and realized that they were unschooled, ordinary men, they were astonished **and they took note that these men had been with Jesus.**" Acts 4:13 (That was the only explanation)

What are some of the ways in which we can demonstrate that we have been with Jesus?

* **Love**—"But I tell you: Love your enemies and pray for those who persecute you." Mt 5:44 "This is my command: Love each other." Jn 15:17 "Love must be sincere" Rom 12:9

+ **Belief/Trust**—Some trust in chariots and some in horses, but we trust in the name of the Lord our God." Ps 21:7

+ **Forgiveness**—". . . forgiving each other, just as in Christ God forgave you." Eph 4:32b "Bear with each other and forgive whatever grievances you may have against one another. Forgive as the Lord forgave you." Col 3:13

+ **Humility**—"All of you clothe yourself with Humility toward one another, because God opposes the proud but gives grace to the humble." 1 Pet 5:5b ". . . in humility consider others better than yourselves." Php 2:3b

+ **Wisdom**—"He who wins souls is wise." Pr 11:30b

+ **Boldness**—"The righteous are as bold as a lion." Pr 28:1b

+ **Courage**—". . . without being frightened in any way by those who oppose you." Php 1:28 'You will not fear the terror of night, nor the arrow that flies by day . . ." Ps 91:5

+ **Faith**—"The righteous will live by faith." Hab 2:4 "Faith is being sure of what we hope for." Heb 11:1 'We live by faith not by sight." 2 Cor 5:7

+ **Prayerfulness/Thankfulness/Joyfulness**—"From inside the fish Jonah prayed." Jnh 2:1 "Be joyful always; pray continually; give thanks in all circumstances." 2 Thes 5:16

+ **Respect**—"Show proper respect to everyone; Love the brotherhood of believers, fear God, honor the king." 1 Pet 2:17

✦ **Living by the word**—"Do not merely listen to the word . . . Do what it says." Ja 1:22

MEMORIZE—"By this all men will know that you are my disciples, if you love one another." Jn 13: 35

IT IS THE LORD

The Lord reveals Himself to us in many different ways. He does that through His word (the Bible), nature, His Ministers, friends, family, circumstances, etc. Unfortunately, we don't always hear Him or recognize His voice right away. It is either because we are not paying attention, we don't believe Him, or we have not learned to recognize His voice or ways. Jesus says in John 10:4b, "and His sheep follow Him because **they know His voice.**" When we fail to recognize His voice we miss out on things like: His encouragement, comfort, assurance, directions, and blessings. Jesus revealed Himself to different individuals after His resurrection. They recognized Him through the things they knew about Him.

Mary Magdalene went to the tomb on the Day of Resurrection, only to discover that it was empty. She reported that to Peter and John, "They have taken the Lord out of the tomb, and we don't know where they have put Him!" Jn 20:2b Peter and John went to verify her story, and after that they left, "but Mary stood outside the tomb crying." Jn 20:11a Jesus appeared to her at the tomb, but she thought He was the gardener. During the conversation, Jesus said to her, "Mary" V16a As soon as she heard the mention of her name, she knew who she had been talking to, **she had recognized His voice.** So "She turned toward Him and cried out in Aramaic, 'Rabboni!'" V 16b Oh, the joy, the excitement, and the peace she must have felt to know that her Lord was alive after all, the result of **voice recognition.** Had she not recognized His voice, she might have continued to sorrow over His death and disappearance from the tomb.

Likewise, when Jesus appeared to the disciples by the sea of Tiberias, they recognized Him, not by His appearance but by what He said and did. They admitted to Him their failure and disappointment for the night. They had not caught any fish. When Jesus told them what to do, and the result was a large catch of fish, they knew right away who He was. John said to Peter, **"It is the Lord."** Jn 21:7b How comforting and how reassuring it might have been for them! Do you ever recognize Him in your circumstances, and are you able to follow His leading? When the disciples did, the result was astonishing.

On the day of resurrection, two disciples were on their way to Emmaus, a village seven miles from Jerusalem. They were discussing the events from the past few days, i.e. Jesus' death and resurrection. As they went along, Jesus went up and walked with them. They didn't recognize Him, even when He rebuked them for being so slow in understanding the Scriptures. They invited Him home to dinner, and at the table, as He took bread, gave thanks, broke it and began to give to them (He had a habit of doing that), their eyes were opened **and they recognized Him.** Luke 24:30-31 Are you able to recognize Him through His ways of doing things? We need to look for God in all situations and circumstances and be able to declare to ourselves and others, **"It is the Lord."**

KEEPING THE TONGUE AND MOUTH UNDER CONTROL

See what Scripture says about the tongue.

We struggle in our work environment to maintain a Godly testimony but very often, and may be, more often than we realize, our tongues get in the way nullifying our testimony.

"Likewise the tongue is a small part of the body, but it makes great boasts. Consider what a great forest is set on fire by a small spark. The tongue also is a fire, a world of evil among the parts of the body. It corrupts the whole person, sets the whole course of his life on fire, and is itself set on fire by hell. All kinds of animals, birds, reptiles and creatures of the sea are being tamed and have been tamed by man, but no man can tame the tongue. It is a restless evil, full of deadly poison. With the tongue we praise our Lord and Father, and with it we curse men, who have been made in God's likeness. Out of the same mouth come praise and cursing. My brothers, this should not be. Can both fresh water and salt water come from the same spring? My brothers, can a fig tree bear olives, or grapevine bear figs? Neither can salt spring produce fresh water." James 3:5-12

""Whoever slanders his neighbor in secret him will I put to silence." Ps 101:5

"When words are many, sin is not absent, but he who holds his tongue is wise.Prov 10 :19

"If anyone considers himself religious and yet does not keep a tight rein on his tongue, he deceives himself and his religion is worthless." James 1:26

"For, whoever would love life and see good days must keep his tongue from evil and his lips from deceitful speech." 1 Peter 3:10

What the tongue and mouth should be doing

"The mouth of the righteous man <u>utters wisdom</u>, and his tongue <u>speaks what is just</u>."
Ps 37:30

"The mouth of the righteous is <u>a fountain of life</u>." Prov 10 :11

"She <u>speaks with wisdom</u>, and <u>faithful instruction </u>is on her tongue." Prov 31:26

"True instruction was in his mouth and <u>nothing false </u>was found on his lips. Mal 2:6

"So that with one heart and mouth you may <u>glorify the God and Father </u>of our Lord Jesus Christ." Rom 15:6

"The lips of the righteous <u>nourish many</u>," Prov10 :21

". . . <u>no lies </u>was found in their mouths; they are blameless." Rev 14 :5

"I will watch my ways and keep my tongue from sin; I will put a <u>muzzle on my mouth as long as the wicked are in my presence."</u> <u>Ps 39:1</u>

"Keep your tongue from evil and your lips from speaking lies" Ps 34 :13

OBEDIENCE

The free online dictionary defines obedience as: 1. To carry out or fulfill a command, order, or instruction. 2. To carry out or comply with a command. The free Merriam Webster gives the following examples of obedience: <The drill sergeant demanded complete and unquestioning obedience from the recruits> <the cowardly obedience with which the dictator's henchmen followed his every command>

God demands obedience from His children, but what does that really mean. I believe it simply means doing what He asks of us or expects of us in a timely manner. What should our attitude be towards obedience? First of all, our obedience should be based on love for God and faith in Him. Knowing that His plans for us are for our good should make us trust and obey Him completely. Jer 11:29 Unlike the above example, our obedience should not be cowardly, but reverential.

If we love and trust him, obedience should be prompt, without question, and carried out to the latter. Abraham demonstrated this type of obedience very well. When God asked him to sacrifice Isaac, he did not ask why, even though he could have reminded God that Isaac was the heir through whom His promises were going to be fulfilled. Also, when Abraham got the orders, he wasted no time to carry it out. The Bible says, **"Early the next morning** Abraham got up and saddled his donkey . . . **he set out** for the place God had told him about." Gen 22:3. On arrival at the designated place, Abraham made the necessary preparations to sacrifice Isaac. Just before he killed the boy, God stopped him. So as we see, Abraham asked no questions, obeyed promptly, and carried out the orders to the latter, believing that God was able to bring him back to life.

King Saul, unlike Abraham, did a half hearted job when God asked him to totally destroy the Amalekites, without exception. 1 Sam 15:3. Disobediently, he spared the king, Agag and the best of the sheep and cattle . . . . everything that was good with the excuse that the soldiers wanted to sacrifice those to the Lord. 1 Sam 15:15. Surprisingly, Saul considered his half-hearted obedience as obedience. He said to Samuel, "But I did obey the Lord. I went on the mission the Lord assigned me . . . Gilgal." V 20. Samuel responded, "Does the Lord delight in burnt offerings and sacrifices as much as in obeying the voice of the Lord? To obey is better than sacrifice, and to heed than the fat of rams." 1 sam 15:22

God promised to bless the Israelites on one condition, obedience: "If you **diligently obey** the voice of the LORD your God, to observe carefully all His commandments which I command you today, then the LORD your God will set you high above all nations of the earth. And all these blessings shall come upon you and **overtake you,** because you obey the voice of the LORD your God: . . . So you shall not turn aside from any of the words which I command you this day, to the right or the left, to go after other gods to serve them." Deut 28:1-14

Whether He blesses us or not when we obey Him, we have to remember that He is God and we have to do as He says!! He does not owe us anything; we owe Him our very lives.

OBEYING GOD NOT FOR PERSONAL GAIN

To obey God is to submit to His command and do things His way, whether or not we understand His reasoning. It takes faith to obey God. Which one of us will give his or her child stone in place of bread or snake instead of a piece of fish? So then, as evil as we are, if we can give good things to our children, we can be assured that God will not give us anything bad. (Mt 7:9-10) Therefore it is safe to trust and obey Him! When God commands, He does not have to explain, but quite often He does. For instance, He said to the Israelites (and us of course), "Honor your father and your mother, **so that** you may live long in the land the LORD your God is giving you." Ex 20:12

Daniel's friends, Shadrach, Meshach and Abednego, when threatened with the hot furnace could have come up with some excuse, bowed and worshiped that ugly image set up by Nebuchadnezzar, and saved their lives. However, they stood their ground and refused to worship the image; God was enough. Good for them! They knew what the king's decree was, but they also knew the power of God and His command that said, "You shall have no other God's before me. You shall not make for yourself an idol in the form of anything in heaven or on earth . . . You shall not bow down to them or worship them." Ex 20:3-5a

They said to the king, "If we are thrown into the blazing furnace, the God we serve is able to save us from it, and He will rescue us from your hand, O king. But even if He does not, we want you to know, O king that we will not serve your gods or worship the image of gold you have set up." Dan 3:17-18

Obeying God does not guarantee the outcome we want or desire in any given situation. God could have chosen to let these men perish in the furnace, even though they were determined to trust and obey Him. It would simply have meant that He had better plans for them. Like the Apostle Paul said, going to be with the Lord is better by far (Php 1:23).

Abraham believed God could bring Isaac back to life even if he killed him in sacrifice, but that was not the reason he took Isaac to the mountain. It was because God asked him to. He was being obedient and leaving the outcome in God's hands. When we obey God, our focus should not be on any particular benefit to us. We need to understanding that the outcome could be very different from our expectations.

Our reasons for obeying should be:

+ He commanded (He said so!)
+ We trust His wisdom, even when we don't understand
+ He has the right and power to do anything the way He wants (He is sovereign)
+ He has plans for us, and they are plans for our welfare, not for evil, to give us a hope and a future. Jer 29:11
+ In all things He works for the good of those who love Him. Rom 8:28

(The good in question will not always be what we have in mind, but good all the same, even better.)

The Hymnist says, "There is no other way to be happy in Jesus but to trust and obey."

LIP SERVICE

(Dictionary definition of lip service—insincere profession of friendship, admiration, support, etc.)

Do our lives reflect what we say we believe? The following need to be evident in our lives:

LOVE THE LORD

"Love the Lord your God with all your heart and with all your soul and with all your mind."
Mt 22: 37

"These people come near to me with their mouth and honor me with their lips, but their hearts are far from me." Isaiah 29:13

"Isaiah was right when he prophesied about you hypocrites; as it is written; "these people honor me with their lips, but their hearts are far from me. They worship me in vain; their teachings are but rules taught by men." Mark 7: 6-7

BE DOERS OF THE WORD / OBEDIENCE

"They claim to know God, but by their actions they deny Him. They are detestable, disobedient and unfit for doing anything good." Titus 1:16

"Do not merely listen to the word, and so deceive yourselves. **Do what it says.**" James 1:22

"Why do you call me 'Lord, Lord,' and do not what I say? Luke 6: 46 (read 46-49)

"You call me 'Teacher' and 'Lord' and rightly so, for that is what I am. Now that I, your Lord and Teacher, have washed your feet, you also should wash one another's feet. I have set you an example that you should do as I have done for you." Jn 13 : 13-15

"You have let go of the commands of God and are holding onto the traditions of men . . . . Thus you nullify the word of God by your tradition that you have handed down. And you do many things like that" Mark 7 : 8-13

DO AS I SAY, BUT ALSO AS I DO

There's an old saying, "Do as I say, not as I do." Jesus however will say, "Do as I say, but also as I do" A dear bible teacher recently wrote, "Jesus will never ask us to do anything He wouldn't do Himself." I therefore took a few minutes to reflect on Jesus' life and teaching, and came to the same conclusion as this bible teacher.

Let's look at a few of those instances.

- ✦ **Forgiveness.** "If you forgive men when they sin against you, your heavenly Father will also forgive you." Mt 6:14 Jesus could have held a grudge against Peter for denying Him and against the disciples for abandoning Him in the garden, but didn't. How about us, with our numerous sins, or the woman caught in adultery? He still loves us unconditionally. At His worst hour, Jesus prayed for forgiveness for His enemies

- ✦ **Prayer.** He didn't only teach us what to say when we pray (Mt 6:5-13); He prayed the same way Himself; always giving thanks to the Father, in all things. He thanked God before breaking the bread and fish for the crowd. He thanked God before calling Lazarus out of the tomb. He didn't only teach us to pray without ceasing, He Himself prayed without ceasing. There were times when He withdrew from everyone else to a quiet place, alone, so He could pray. Before He selected the twelve, He spent all night praying. O that we might learn to pray so earnestly!

+ **Fasting.** In Mt 17, after the disciples could not heal a lunatic, Jesus explained to them, "Howbeit this kind goeth not out but by prayer and fasting." V 21 Did He say that just to deprive us of food? Certainly not! He fasted forty days, for a good reason. The devil came to tempt Him after that, but failed miserably because Jesus was more than ready for him. Let's take this challenge seriously. Food isn't going to go anywhere; it will wait for us till we are ready. This week's challenge—At least half a day fast with focus on prayer; we can do it!

+ **Supporting others.** "Rejoice with those who rejoice; mourn with those who mourn." Rom 12:15 Jesus was at the wedding at Cana in Galilee, sharing their joy, and even provided more wine to make the occasion a success. Jn 2:1-8 He went to see Mary and Martha when they lost their brother Lazarus. Jn 11:35

+ **Intercession.** The word teaches us to pray for one another. Jesus said to Peter, "Simon, Simon, Satan has asked to sift you as wheat. **But I have prayed for you,** Simon that your faith may not fail." Lk 22:31-32a

+ **Humility.** Jesus, being God, humbled Himself to the point of death, even death on the cross. Although He was Lord, and should be served, He washed the disciples' feet. Jn 13:4-5 He told them He was setting an example for them. Jn 13:14-15 He cooked breakfast for them on the beach. Jn21:9-12a Why didn't He wait for them to cook their own fish? Again, He was setting the example and also meeting their physical need. (they had worked all night; they were tired and hungry).

+ **Praise seeking.** "But when you give to the needy, do not let your left hand know what your right hand is doing." Mt 6:3 "But when you fast, do not look somber as the hypocrites do . . . . Mt 6:16-18 A woman once called out to Jesus saying, "Blessed is the mother who gave birth and nursed you." Jesus replied, "Blessed rather are those who hear the word of God and obey it." Lk 11:27-28

+ **Death.** Many Christians, from the early church and even the present have lost their lives following Christ. Missionaries have lost their lives because of hostility from the very natives they were trying to help, or through sickness. But let's remember, Jesus was the **FIRST** to die for the faith!

Is there anything that Jesus has asked us to do that He didn't do?

MEMORIZE: "Take my yoke upon you and learn from me, for I am gentle and humble in heart, and you will find rest for your souls." Mt 11:29

CHRISTIANS ARE CALLED TO BE:

CHILDREN OF GOD
'To all who received Him, to those who believed in His name, He gave the right to become the children of God." Jn 1:12

"You are all sons of God through faith in Christ Jesus." Gal 3:26

How then should we behave as children? LOVE, REVERE, OBEY, and SERVE Him.

FAMILY OF GOD/ BODY OF CHRIST/ CHURCH/HOUSEHOLD OF FAITH
"So in Christ we who are many form one body, and each member belongs to all the others." Rom 12:5

"Now you are the body of Christ, and each one is a part of it." 1 Cor 12:27

"Therefore, as we have opportunity, let us do good to all people, especially to those who belong to the family of believers." Gal 6:10

AMBASSADORS
"We are therefore Christ's ambassadors, as though God were making His appeal through us." 2 Cor 5:20 (Representing Christ in all we do and say)

LIGHT
"You are the light of the world. A city on a hill cannot be hidden. Neither do people light a lamp and put it under a bowl. Instead they put it on a stand, and it gives light to everyone in the house.

In the same way, let your light shine before men, that they may see your good deeds, and praise your Father in heaven." Mt 5:14-16

SALT
"You are the salt of the earth. But if the salt loses its saltiness, how can it be made salty again? It is no longer good for anything, except to be thrown out and trampled by men." Mt 5:13

SOUL WINNERS
"Come follow me and I will make you fishers of men." Mk 1:17

"Therefore go and make disciples of all nations . . ." Mt 28:19

PRIESTS / INTERCESSORS
"With this in mind, be alert and always keep on praying for all the saints (Christians)." Eph 6:18b

"Therefore, confess your sins to each other and pray for each other so that you may be healed. The prayer of a righteous man is powerful and effective." Ja 5:16

"Brothers, pray for us." 1 Th 5:25

MEMORY VERSE: "Brothers, pray for us." 1 th 5;25
Any time you say that verse, pray for someone

OMISSIONS, JUST AS IMPORTANT

Christians know the importance of prayer. That is our way of communicating with our Father. We are able to express our adoration and love for Him; we express our shame and remorse for our sins and ask for forgiveness. We petition Him for our needs, and intercede on behalf of others and on behalf of our world.

When we offer petitions and intercessions, we seek a response from the One to whom we've prayed. He could answer in one of many different ways like: okay, no, wait; you got to be kidding, are you okay? or return to the drawing board, etc. Whether we like His answers or not they are still answers; He has clearly communicated His intentions.

Although He loves us and desires to provide for us, the bible tells us there are times when our prayers don't make it to his ears. Some of the reasons are:

+ <u>Sins:</u> The Psalmist says, "If I had cherished sin in my heart, the Lord would not have listened; but God has surely listened and heard my voice in prayer." Ps 66: 18-19

+ <u>Lack of faith:</u> "According to your faith will it be done to you." Mt 9:29 "The prayer offered in faith will make the sick well; the Lord will raise him up." Ja 5:15a

+ <u>Wrong motives</u>: "You do not have, because you do not ask God. When you ask, you do not receive, because you ask with wrong motives." Ja 4:2b-3a

- **God's Will**; "This is the confidence we have in approaching God: that if we ask anything according to His will, He hears us." 1 Jn 5:14

Quite often when we think about repentance, we are referring to committed sins, and we should, but there is more. The sin of omission is when we neglect to carry out God's commands; it affects our relationship with Him the same way our committed sins do. Unfortunately, the sin of omission does not get quite as much attention. God's response to omissions is the same as to commissions, because both are sins. Let us remind ourselves of some of the times He has expressed concern over omissions.

- "Woe to you teachers . . . you hypocrites! You give a tenth of your spices-mint, dill . . . But you have <u>neglected</u> the more important matters of the law-justice, mercy and faithfulness. You should have practiced the latter, without <u>neglecting</u> the former." Mt 23:23

- "Is it a time for you yourselves to be living in your paneled houses, while this House (the temple) <u>remains</u> a ruin?" Haggai 1:4

- "I was hungry and you <u>gave me nothing</u> to eat, I was thirsty and you <u>gave me nothing</u> to drink, I was a stranger and you <u>did not invite</u> me in, . . . I was sick and in prison and you <u>did not look after</u> me." Mt 25:42-43

May the Lord make us increasingly aware of the responsibilities we are neglecting, and may we be penitent about them as we should.

OPPORTUNE TIMES

One of the accounts of Jesus' temptation by the devil in the wilderness is recorded in the gospel of Luke (vs. 1-13). Verse 13 says, "When the devil had finished all this tempting, he left Him until an opportune time." Synonyms for opportune are: fitting, appropriate, favorable, apt, right, suitable, and timely. The devil withdrew from Jesus after he had failed, but didn't give up. He planned to return to try again when the time would hopefully **be just right for him to succeed**. It was so prideful of the devil to think that he could succeed in making Jesus disobey God. He must have miscalculated the distance Jesus was willing to go to please His Father! Jesus cannot sin! Amen!

What are opportune times? Opportune times are the instances when it is the easiest to achieve one's goals, or when one's efforts are most successful. For the devil, the enemy of our soul, those are the times when we Christians are at our weakest, when we let down our guard, not being watchful, when we are not praying or studying the word or when we are not living according to the word, or when we fail to set boundaries. We can set boundaries by deciding what our responses would be before we are ever in certain situations. Like Daniel who resolved not to defile himself with the Babylonian king's meat and wine before it was offered to him (Dan 1:8). Can you think of an instance when you made a bad choice or decision because you hadn't set any boundaries before hand?

The devil's strategy of waiting for an opportune time wouldn't have worked with Jesus any way, but how about us? Hasn't that strategy worked repeatedly with us? Sadly, the answer is "Yes". When the devil prowls around like a roaring lion looking for someone to devour (1 Peter 5:8), he is looking for an opportune time, and sad to say he finds it time and time again. The word admonishes us to "Submit yourselves, then to God. Resist the devil, and he will flee from you." Ja 4:7

Although the devil flees when we resist him, he does return, with the hope of finding an opportune time. We need to be consistently submitted to God so that we can deny him those opportune times. That is why the word warns us to "Watch and pray so that you will not fall into temptation." Mt 26:41 "Our struggle is not against flesh and blood, but against the rulers, against the authorities, against the powers of this dark world and against the spiritual forces of evil in the heavenly realms" Eph 6:12 (In the wilderness, Jesus was not faced with flesh and blood). The key to denying the devil these opportune times is to "Put on the whole armor of God, so that when the day of evil comes, you may be able to stand your ground." Eph 6:14 Putting on the armor is the beginning, but we have to keep it on day and night. Taking it off creates an opportune time for the devil, and before we know it, we have become victims instead of victors. The hymnist admonishes us to gird our heavenly armor on, to wear it ever night and day, for ambush lies the evil one, so watch and pray, watch and pray.

INFORMATION AND YOU

Information helps us to make decisions that could make us or break us, and it comes to us from many different sources: from books, the media, politicians, individuals, and from the Bible. As Christians, the only trust-worthy source is the Bible. When we receive information, we are compelled to take action or respond in some fashion. We may choose to disregard it, because we don't believe it or don't find it useful or we may actually use the information in a positive way and pass it on to others. Unfortunately, the information we choose to disregard, sometimes is really information we need to use.

The information we receive benefits us, others or both; in either case we need to take some action. If we intentionally disregard information that would benefit us, we do that to our own detriment, and if we don't pass it on to others who might benefit from it, we do them a disservice.

Having said all that, what have you done with all that you've read from the Bible? Is the word of God gradually changing your life or are you the same old person? For example, has "Thou shall not steal." made any difference in your life, or are you still stealing and making excuses? Are you bringing supplies home from work or have you stopped? How about, "Work out your own salvation with fear and trembling." Are you taking your Christian walk seriously? Becoming a Christian is just the beginning. We need to stay alert, study the Word, resist the devil and press on in the power of the Spirit, so that we will not fall prey to the devil and sin, but instead our lives will be transformed as the Word of God renews our minds. If our lives are not being transformed by the Word, this is what James says, 'Anyone who listens to the word but does not do what it says is like a man who looks at his face in a mirror and, after looking at himself, goes away and immediately forgets what he looks like." Ja 1:23-24

On the other hand if we obey what we read or hear, James goes on to say, "But the man who looks intently into the perfect law that gives freedom, and continues to do this, not forgetting what he has heard, but doing it-he will be blessed in what he does." Ja 1:25

These days, everyone is looking at the signs of the times, including unbelievers, and thinking "The Lord's coming is close." Of course we don't know the exact time, but we believe it's closer than when we first believed. The Apostle Peter puts it this way, "But the day of the Lord will come like a thief. The heavens will disappear with a roar; the elements will be destroyed by fire, and the earth and everything in it will be laid bare. **Since everything will be destroyed in this way, what kind of people ought ye to be? You ought to live holy and godly lives." 2 Pet 3:10-11**

Since His coming is so close and everything is going to be destroyed anyway, what should be our attitude towards **THINGS?** John says it this way, "Do not **love** the world or anything in the world, if anyone loves the world, the love of the Father is not in him . . . The world and its desires pass away, but the man who does the will of God lives forever." 1 Jn 2:15-17 On the brighter side, Jesus says, "In my Father's house are many mansions, if it were not so, I would have told you. I am going there to prepare a place for you." Jn 14:1-2

What should our attitude be towards the unsaved? David says in Ps 7:11, "God is angry with the wicked every day." (Scary) John says in Jn 3:36, "Whoever believes in the Son has eternal life, but whoever rejects the Son will not see life, for God's wrath remains on him." We need to warn folks the same way we would when the weather forecast is bad and a bad storm is expected. People are sometimes evacuated to ensure no one is hurt. The Apostle Paul puts it this way, "Knowing therefore the terror of the Lord, we persuade men . . ." 2 Cor 5:11a

So we see we have enough information to admonish us to live godly lives, and to warn the unbeliever to turn to Christ for salvation. Information is not very helpful until it motivates us to take the right action.

FAITH VS WORKS

We come to God through faith in Christ. Salvation is not by merit or the rewards of good works. The Bible clearly says "For it is by grace you have been saved, through faith-and this not from yourselves, it is the gift of God-not by works, so that no one can boast."

Eph 2:8-9. So it is evident that salvation is by grace through faith.

However we are saved to do good works. "For we are God's workmanship, created in Christ Jesus to do good works, which God prepared in advance for us to do." Eph 2:10 People determine what we are by our actions and not only by what we say. When our works contradict our claims, we plant doubt in people's minds.

WHAT IS "GOOD WORKS"

Works—Deeds; Efforts. (Dictionary definition)
Good Works—Faith in action; the non-verbal expression of faith; expressing faith without verbally saying, "I am a Christian." (Pearl's definition)

HOW DO WE EXPRESS GOOD WORKS?

I. **Serving God**
    "Love the Lord your God with all your heart and with all your soul and with all your strength." Deut 6:5 We show this love through reverence, worship, faith/trust, dependence on Him, and obedience.

    "And now, O Israel, what does the Lord your God ask of you but to fear the Lord your God, to walk in all His ways, to love Him, to serve the Lord your God with all your heart and with all your soul, and to observe the Lord's commands and decrees." Deut 10:12-13a

2. Serving others

"... love your neighbor as yourself..." Mt 22:39b

"Finally, all of you, live in harmony with one another; be sympathetic, love as brothers, be compassionate and humble. Do not repay evil with evil or insult with insult, but with blessing, because to this you were called so that you may inherit a blessing." 1 Pet 3:8-9

"What good is it, my brothers, if a man claims to have faith but have no deeds? Can such faith save him?" James 2:14 (read 14-26)

"As the body without the spirit is dead, so faith without works is dead." Ja 2:26

"Live such good lives among the pagans that, though they accuse you of doing wrong, they may see your good deeds and glorify God on the day He visits us." 1 Pet 2:12

"Therefore, as we have opportunity, let us do good to all people, especially to those who belong to the family of believers." Gal 6:10

"But the fruit of the spirit is love, joy, peace, patience, kindness, goodness, faithfulness, gentleness and self control." Gal 5:22-23b

HOW ABOUT APPLICATION IN THE WORKPLACE?

"Let your light shine before men, that they may see your good deeds and praise your Father in heaven." Mt 5:16 (memorize)

OUR POSITION IN CHRIST

Below is a partial list of what we are in Christ. It is exciting what He has made of us and also called us to be. As we rejoice in our position, let us also remember that the position comes with responsibilities. First and foremost is to love the Lord with all our hearts, with all our strength . . . and to love our neighbors. If we love the Lord, we will obey Him, "If you love me you will obey what I command." Jn 14:15. This is love for God; to obey His commands." 1 Jn 5:3. That will bring noticeable changes in our lives.

These changes will influence our environment for Christ. "But thanks be to God, who always leads us in triumphal procession in Christ and through us spread everywhere the fragrance of the knowledge of Him. For we are to God the aroma of Christ among those who are being saved and those who are perishing. To the one we are the smell of death; to the other, the fragrance of life." 2 Cor 2: 14-16b

LOVED "For God so loved the world that He gave His only Son, that whoever believes in Him shall not perish but have everlasting life." Jn 3:16

FORGIVEN   "As far as the east is from the west, so far has he removed our transgressions from us." Ps 103:12

SANCTIFIED   "For them I sanctify myself, that they too may be truly sanctified. Jn 17:19

HEIRS   "Now if we are children, then we are heirs—heirs of God and co-heirs with Christ, if indeed we share

74

in His sufferings in order that we may also share in His glory." Rom 8:17

SEALED "He anointed us, set His seal of ownership on us and put His spirit in our hearts as a deposit, guaranteeing what is to come." 2 Cor 1:21b-22

CHOSEN "But you are a chosen people, a royal priesthood, a holy nation, a people

PRIESTS belonging to God, that you may declare the praises of Him who called you

HOLY out of darkness into His wonderful light." 1 Pet 2-9

BELONGING TO GOD

SAINT/JUDGES "Do you not know that the saints will judge the world? . . . Do you not know that we will judge angels?" 1 Cor 6:2-3

MEMORIZE "He anointed us, set His seal of ownership on us and put His spirit in our hearts as a deposit, <u>guaranteeing</u> what is to come." 2 Cor 1: 21b-22

OWNERSHIP PART I

"The earth is the Lord's, and everything in it, the world, and all who live in it; for He founded it upon the seas and established it upon the waters." Ps 24:1-2

Why is the earth the Lord's?

Because He created it, He called it into being. "In the beginning God created the heavens and the earth." Gen 1:1 "And God said, "Let there be . . ." Gen 1:3, 6, 9, 11, 14, 20,

How does one become an owner of something?

1. Buying it.
2. Creating or making it.
3. Receiving it as a gift

What are some of the privileges of ownership?

1. Have the title to the property "the earth is the Lord's." Ps 24:1
2. Do with it as you please. "Now the Lord God had planted a garden in the east, in Eden; and there He put the man He had formed."
3. Give it to whomever you please "Then God said, 'I give you every seed-bearing plant . . . . and to all the beasts of the earth . . . . I give you every green plant for food.'" Gen 1:29-30a
4. Destroy it whenever and however. "I am going to bring floodwaters on the earth to destroy all life under the

heavens, every creature that has the breath of life in it. Everything on earth will perish." Gen 6:17. Every living thing that *moved* on the earth perished-birds, livestock, wild animals, all the creatures that swam over the earth, and all mankind. Everything on dry land that had the breath of life in its nostrils died." Gen 7:21-22

We are God's because:

1. *He created us.* "I praise you because I am fearfully and wonderfully **made**;" Ps139:14a. "This is what the Lord says—He who **formed** you in the womb, and who will help you;" Isaiah 44:2
2. *He purchased* us at a price, the blood of His Son, "Fear not, for I have redeemed you; I have summoned you by name; **YOU ARE MINE.**" Isaiah 43: 1b
3. *A Gift to Christ—*" I have revealed you to those whom you gave me out of the world. They were yours; you gave them to me and they have obeyed your word." Jn 17:6

If we are God's then:

1. *He can do with us as He pleases*, "Yet, O Lord, you are our Father. We are the clay, you are the potter;" Is 64:8a. "Like clay in the hand of the potter, so are you in my hand, O house of Israel." Je 18:6b.
2. *We should not question His judgment.* "Woe to him who quarrels with his maker, to him who is but a potsherd among the potsherds on the ground. Does the clay say to the potter, 'what are you making?'" Is 45:9 ". . . do you question me about my children, or give me orders about the work of my hands?' Is 45:11b. "But who are you, O man, to talk back to God? Shall what is formed say to Him who formed it, 'Why did you make me like this?'" Rom 9:20

MEMORIZE *"You are mine" Is 43:1b*

OWNERSHIP PART II

After establishing that it is foolish to question God's judgment, it is important to also note the difference between questioning God and acknowledging pain and discomfort.

Questioning God's judgment will be; thinking, feeling or asking something like, "why will God do something like that? It would have been better to do it some other way."

It reminds me of the woman who anointed Jesus' head with the expensive perfume. "When the disciples saw this they were indignant, 'why this waste?' they asked. This perfume could have been sold at a high price and the money given to the poor." Mt 26:8-9

Jesus' response, "Why are you bothering this woman? She has done a beautiful thing to me. The poor you will always have with you, but you will not always have me. When she poured this perfume on my body, she did it to prepare me for burial." Mt 26:10-12

Acknowledging pain and discomfort is totally different. On the cross, Jesus cried to the Father, "My God, my God, why have you forsaken me?" Mt 27:46 And even before then, in the garden He cried, "My Father, if it is possible, may this cup be taken from me. Yet not as I will, but as you will." Mt 26:39

If Jesus admitted pain and apprehension, we can too, but in our admission, we should be careful not to think or feel God made a mistake. Our pain or discomfort should draw us closer to God, and if for some reason we don't feel His presence, let us call out like Jesus did, "why have you forsaken me?" Even in those painful situations, let's remember that, "In all things God works for the good of those who love Him, who have been called according to His purpose." Rom 8:28

So in our troubles, let us encourage one another to focus on the Lord, because He does have a plan for each of us, and it's not always going to be pain-free. He is so good, He makes sure we are not all down or discouraged at the same time. It is difficult to focus properly when one is down, but a word of encouragement from a friend is all it takes to get us back on track. Let us continue to pray for each other.

God has a right to do with us as He pleases, but His plans for us are plans for welfare not for evil, to give us each a future and hope.

IMPORTANCE OF CHRISTIAN FELLOWSHIP

Fellow-A member of learned or professional group (dictionary definition)

Fellowship—a group of people with the same belief and purpose. (Pearl's def)

Therefore, **Christian Fellowship** will be a gathering of Christians. The meeting place is irrelevant; it could be in a church hall, someone's home etc. "For where two or three come together in my name, there am I with them." Mt 18:20

PURPOSE OF CHRISTIAN FELLOWSHIP

We are **encouraged to** do so—"Let us not give up meeting together, as some are in the habit of doing, but let us encourage one another." Heb 10:25

Ministering to each other through our gifts and talents. The Lord reveals different things to different people. Therefore, when we come together to share, be it a Bible study or prayer meeting, we walk away at the end with more insight and encouragement than what we came with individually. "For you can all prophecy in turn so that everyone may be instructed and encouraged." 1 Cor 14:31

God responds to the fellowship of His children—"then those who feared the Lord talked with each other, and the Lord listened and heard." Mal 3:16

Power in group prayer—Peter had been in jail, the angel of the Lord set him free, he went to the house of Mary, John Mark's mother, "where many people had gathered and were praying." Acts 12:12

I believe their prayer had a lot to do with Peter's release.

Following the example of the early church ("All scripture is . . . and is useful for teaching, rebuking, correcting and training in righteousness." 2Tim 3:16) If fellowship worked for them, it should work for us. "They devoted themselves to the apostles' teaching and to the fellowship, to the breaking of bread and to prayer." Acts 2:42

RESULTS OF CHRISTIAN FELLOWSHIP

We are encouraged
We learn
We grow
We see results
We are corrected
We are trained in righteousness
God is honored

LOVING THE BRETHREN

WHO IS THE BRETHREN? (Christians, the church, the body of Christ)

<u>DISCIPLE</u>—a follower, particularly one who follows Jesus Christ (dictionary def)

"And the disciples were called Christians first in Antioch." Acts 11:26b

Therefore Christian=Disciple of Christ

WHY SHOULD WE LOVE THE BRETHREN?

Jesus commanded it, and it is proof of discipleship
"A new command I give you: Love one another. <u>As I have loved you</u>, so you must love one another. By this all men will know that you are my disciples, if you love one another." Acts 13:35-36
"My command is this: Love each other <u>as I have loved you</u>." Jn 15:12

HOW SHOULD WE LOVE (as Christ loved us)

<u>SINCERITY</u>—"Love must be sincere: be devoted to one another in brotherly love. Honor one another above yourselves." Ro 12:9-10

<u>ABOUNDING</u> . . . . "May the Lord make your love increase and overflow for each other and for everyone else, just as ours does for you." 1 Thes 3:12

<u>DEEPLY</u>—". . . Love one another deeply from the heart." 1Pet 1:22b

"God can testify how I long for all of you with the affection of Jesus Christ." Php 1:8

RESULTS OF BROTHERLY LOVE

1. God is glorified "This is to my Father's glory, that you bear much fruit, showing yourselves to be my Disciples." Jn 15:8
2. Our friendship with Christ is confirmed "You are my friends if you do what I command you." Jn 15:14
3. The needs of the body are met because we pray, give, and support each other as needed.
   "Let us not love with words or tongue but with actions and in truth." 1Jn 3:18 (read11-19)

MEMORY VERSE "Whoever does not love, does not know God, because God is love."1 Jn 4:8

Quietly before the Lord, let us individually try to answer these questions:

1. How has Christ loved me? (We have to know how, because He wants us to love as He loved us.)

2. How can I show love to my brethren? (When we find out, let's put it into action)

MIND YOUR OWN BUSINESS

Do you ever consider in your heart to say, or have you actually said to another person, "Mind your own business"? Most of us have at one time or another said it or thought it, but the truth is, our business is each other's business. The reason being, our actions have ramifications. They affect God, other Christians, unbelievers and the Church as a whole.

How it affects God

1. Dishonoring God. "Because by doing this you have made the enemies of the Lord show utter contempt . . ." 2 Sam 12:14 (this was regarding David's sin with Bathsheba)
2. "God's name is blasphemed among the Gentiles because of you." Rom 2:24

How it affects other Christians

1. Christians are stereotyped. Can you recall an instance when a Christian is hated or criticized because of another Christian's behavior? It happens quite often.
2. Younger Christians are confused and discouraged, and even misled. "When Peter came to Antioch, I opposed him to his face, because he was clearly in the wrong . . . so that by his hypocrisy even Barnabas was led astray." Gal 2:11-13
3. Consider also Rom 14

How innocent people are affected

1. Because of David's sin of adultery, Uriah lost his life. "Put Uriah in the front line where the fighting is fiercest. Then withdraw from him so he will be struck down and die." 2 Sam 11:15
2. David's first son with Bathsheba died through no fault of his own. "But because ... the son born to you will die." 2 Sam 12:14
3. How about Achan's family and cattle? His whole family, including his cattle died because his covetousness led him to steal, bringing judgment on others. Jos 7
4. Seven of Saul's grand children were killed because of the evil he committed years earlier. Prior to that, the Israelites suffered three years of famine for the same reason. 2 Sam 21

How unbelievers are affected

1. There are many unbelievers who turn a deaf ear to the gospel because they are disappointed by the behavior of Christians they know. In other words Christians can get in the way of unbelievers' salvation.
2. Not only do they choose to remain unsaved but they speak ill of God and the Church. They spread their ill feeling against the Church among other unbelievers who in turn choose to stay away from the Church.

How the Church is affected

1. The Church is not as effective as it should be in fulfilling the Great Commission.
2. The Church is targeted for criticism and persecution.
3. It is seen by some unbelievers as a joke, bringing it to a position of weakness rather than the position of power and authority for which God has established it.

The next time you think to say, "Mind your own business!" Remember if you are in the wrong, others are going to be affected sooner or later. Saul was not alive when his grandchildren suffered.

CHRISTIANS' RESPONSIBILITIES TOWARDS EACH OTHER

BUILDING UP

"Do not let any unwholesome talk come out of your mouths, but only what is helpful for building others up according to their needs, that it may benefit those who listen." Eph 4:29

"Everything is permissible-but not everything is beneficial. Everything is permissible-but not everything is constructive. Nobody should seek his own good but the good of others." 1 Cor 10:23-24

"Let us therefore make every effort to do what leads to peace and mutual edification. Do not destroy the work of God for the sake of . . . ." Rom 14:19-20

LOVING

"Keep on loving each other as brothers. Do not . . . ." Heb 13:1-3

"Now that you have purified yourselves by obeying the truth so that you have sincere love for your brothers, love one another deeply, from the heart." 1 Peter 1:22

"Show proper respect to everyone: Love the brotherhood of believers, fear God, honor the king." 1 Peter 2:17

FORGIVING

"Bear with each other and forgive whatever grievances you may have against one another. Forgive as the Lord forgave you." Col 3:13

SHARING EACH OTHERS BURDENS and JOYS

"Carry each other's burdens, and in this way you will fulfill the law of Christ." Gal 6: 2

"Rejoice with those who rejoice; mourn with those who mourn." Rom 12: 15

PRAYING FOR EACH OTHER

"Therefore confess your sins to each other and pray for each other so that you may be healed. The prayer of a righteous man is powerful and effective." James 5:16

BEING AN EXAMPLE

"Do not . . . . , but be an example for the believers in speech, in life, in love, in faith and in purity." 1 Tim 4:12

REBUKE/CORRECTING

"Preach the word; be prepared in season and out of season; correct, rebuke and encourage—with great patience and careful instruction" 2 Tim 4:2

GOD IS TRUSTWORTHY

Trust—(dictionary def. Reliance on a person's integrity, justice, etc.
Worthy—(dictionary def. Deserving)
So to say; God is trustworthy is to say, God deserves to be trusted

WHY GOD IS TRUSTWORTHY

1. **He is God**—"I am the first and the last; apart from me there is no God . . . . You are my witnesses, Is there any God besides me? No, there is no other Rock; I know not one." Isaiah 44:6-8

2. **He keeps His word**—"The one who calls you is faithful and He will do it." 1 Thes 5:24
    "By faith Abraham, even though he was past age—and Sarah herself was barren—was enabled to become a father because *he considered Him faithful who had made the promise." Heb 11:11*

3. **He has power to accomplish what he promises** "All power in heaven and on earth has been given to me." Mt 28:18

BECAUSE HE IS TRUSTWORTHY WE SHOULD:

1. **Trust His word completely, ie. Without doubt.** "Do not let your hearts be troubled. Trust in God; trust also

in me. In my Father's house are many rooms; *if it were not so, I would have told you. Jn 14:1-2*

2. **Trust in the face of pain and suffering** "Be joyful in hope, patient in affliction, faithful in prayer." Rom 12:12

3. **Trust in the face of apparent delay.** "Lord," Martha said to Jesus, "if you had been here, my brother would not have died. But I know that even now God will give you whatever you ask." Jn 11:21

OUR PRAYERS SEEM TO FALL ON DEAF EARS BECAUSE:

1. His timing is very different from ours. "The Lord is not slow in keeping His promise, as some understand slowness." 2 Pet 3:9a (He always has a good reason)

2. He is teaching us patience and perseverance and a few other things. "You need to persevere so that when you have done the will of God, you will receive what He has promised." Heb 10:36

3. He is testing our faith "Jesus loved Martha and her sister and Lazarus. Yet when He heard that Lazarus was sick, He stayed where He was two more days." Jn 11:5

So if the promises you claim are not fulfilled right away, do not give up. Continue to trust.

BE CONSISTENT

I was relieved when we finally bade winter goodbye. I was glad to see spring arrive and kept hoping that it will get warmer and warmer. But even though spring has been around for a few weeks now; it has not warmed up consistently with the passing of time. Rather, the warm has been alternating with the cold. I've tried not to turn on the heat but finally, two days ago, the house being just too cold; I gave in, I turned it on! Just for a day.

The alternating temperature changes make me miserable, and I seldom feel appropriately dressed. When I go outside in warm clothes, I feel too warm and when I go out dressed in light clothes I feel too cold. Why can't it get warm and stay warm? Why should I turn on the heat in almost mid May? I find it very frustrating. So I hope I won't complain when it finally gets hot.

This experience with inconsistency reminds me of how God feels about lukewarm Christians. He said to the church in Laodicea, "I know your deeds, that you are neither cold nor hot. I wish you were either one or the other! So, because you are lukewarm-neither hot nor cold—I am about to spit you out of my mouth" Rev 3:15-16.

This is an indication that God wants us to have a consistent walk with Him and to be growing day by day, by being in the word, doing what it says and praying without ceasing.

With the concept of inconsistency also comes double mindedness. James 1:6-8 tells us a double minded person is unstable in all he does. We are admonished to believe and not doubt when we ask God for wisdom (anything). He is the same

God who created the world with the word of His mouth. God's power is not demonstrated in degrees or percentages. Power is power! Through it He healed the sick raised the dead, turned water into blood, water into wine, raised Christ from the dead and defied gravity when Jesus ascended into heaven. So now, is there anything too hard for Him? No! Why then do we have doubts when we pray?

We find it easier to trust God with less difficult things, and when it comes to overwhelming problems our faith does not measure up. We seem to say to God, "I don't know about this, God, are you up to this challenge?" But the truth is, **<u>nothing</u>** is too hard for the Lord. Gen 18:14a

Since nothing is too hard for the Lord, we need to trust Him completely, all the time, and not just some of the time. Regardless of the circumstances, God can be trusted.

A newborn cries when he/she needs something, and does not concern himself or herself with how the parents are going to meet that need.

Let's learn from the newborn (child); ask for everything we need and trust that everything we need will be provided for by our heavenly Father.

WHY BE GOOD?

After all, we are saved by grace and not by works, so what does it matter?

HIS PURPOSE FOR US-

"For we are God's workmanship, created in Christ Jesus to do good works, which God prepared in advance for us to do." Eph 2 :10

HE COMMANDS US—

"A new command I give you, love one another" Jn 13:34

"Be ye holy because I, the Lord your God, am holy." Lev. 19:2

PROOF OF OUR LOVE FOR CHRIST-

"If you love me, you will obey what I Command." Jn 14:15

"But the world must learn that I love the Father and that I do **exactly** what my Father has commanded me." Jn 14:31(proof that He Loved the Father)

"Whoever has my commands and obeys them, he is the one who loves me. He who loves me will be loved by my Father, . . ." Jn 14:21

"If any man loves me, he will obey my teaching." Jn 14:23

"You are my friends If you do what I command you." Jn 15:14

"This is love for God: to obey His commands." 1 Jn 5:3a

PROOF OF HIS INDWELLING-

"Those who obey his commands live in Him and He in them." 1 Jn 3:24a

FOLLOWING HIS EXAMPLE-

"Take my yoke upon you and learn from me, for I am gentle and humble in heart." Mt 11:29

"I have set you an example that you should do as I have done for you." Jn 13:15

"To this you were called, because Christ suffered for you, leaving you an example that you should follow in His steps." 1 Peter 2:21

"Be imitators of God, therefore, as dearly loved children." Eph 5:1

WE ARE BEING TRANSFORMED-
(the process of change starts at conversion)
"Do not conform any longer to the pattern of this world, but be transformed by the renewing of you mind. Then you will be able to test and approve what God's will is—his good, pleasing and perfect will." Rom 12:2

WE HAVE TO GIVE AN ACCOUNT—

"So then, each of us will give an account of himself to God." Rom14:12

"For we must all appear before the judgment seat of Christ, that each one may receive what is due him for the things done while in the body, whether good or bad." 2 Cor 5:10

TO RECEIVE REWARDS-

"And if anyone gives even a cup of cold water to one of these little ones because he is my disciple, I tell you the truth, he will certainly not lose his reward." Mt 10:42

"But love . . . . then your reward will be great," Lk 6:35

IT SETS US APART / CONVINCES OTHERS

"A new command I give you, love one another. By this all men will know that you are my disciples, if you love one another." Jn 13:34-35

"For a tree is recognized by its fruit." Mt 12:33b

"By their fruit you will recognize them." Mt 7:16, 20

BEING AN ENCOURAGER

To encourage means to inspire, to help.

In our Christian walk we do come face to face with discouraging situations like, sickness, inter-relational issues, finances, falling into sin, etc . . . During those times, we need encouragement from each other. When we encourage, we help the other person to:

+ **Be hopeful—**

  "Moses answered the people, 'Do not be afraid, stand firm and **you will see** the deliverance the Lord will bring you today.'" Ex 14:13

+ **Trust God's promises—**

  "For **I am the Lord,** your God, who takes hold of your right hand and says to you, Do not fear; I will help you." Isa 41:13

+ **Be fearless—**

  "**Don't be afraid**, the prophet answered, Those who are with us are more than those who are with them." 2 Kings 6:16

+ **Press on—**"But as for you be strong, and **do not give up**, for your work will be rewarded." 2Chr 15:7

+ **Cheer up—**"These things I have spoken unto you that in me you might have peace, in the world ye shall have tribulation,: but **be of good cheer**; I have overcome the world." Jn 16:33

+ **Be strong in taking a stand even when opposition is strong—**

"The following night the Lord stood near Paul and said, 'take courage! As you have testified about me in Jerusalem, so you must also testify in Rome'." Acts 23:11

How to encourage each other:

1. put one's self in the other person's place. (What will make you feel hopeful?)
2. Be sensitive (imagine what she is going through and choose your words carefully)
3. Be a good listener
4. Be patient
5. Be non-judgmental
6. Be understanding
7. Be honest
8. Be prayerful

No matter what our individual struggles are, let us remember, "For our struggle is not against flesh and blood, but against the rulers, against the authorities, against the powers of this dark world and against the spiritual forces of evil in the heavenly realms. Therefore, put on the full armor of God, so that when the day of evil comes, you may be able to stand your ground, and after you have done everything, to stand" Eph 6:12-13

DOING IT GOD'S WAY

Commands and counsel, what do they have in common and how do they differ? Both come from another, outside ourselves, and both have consequences. God gives both commands and admonishing in his word. When He commands us, He expects us to go and do exactly what he had asked us to do. There are no ifs, buts, maybes, or later about it. When we choose to disobey Him, we can incur His wrath, and lose the blessing that comes with obedience. He will get another to accomplish that task, and if nobody would, He is able to raise even the rocks to do it. Other times He will insist, and see to it that we do it. Jonah is a good example. God could have delegated someone else to go when Jonah refused to go, but He didn't. Jonah learned his lesson the hard way; he went kicking and screaming. He learned that when God says, "Go." You go. Did God ask for his input, suggestions, or ideas? No! Did God say to Jonah, "Would you like to go to Nineveh, or "Jonah, how about going to Nineveh? No, He just said, "Go" So Jonah learned obedience the hard way, from the belly of the big fish he repented, and when back on shore, he went to do as he was commanded. How about Adam and Eve? They blatantly disobeyed. God didn't say to them, "Eat any fruit you want from the garden." He said "Do not" They were commanded not to eat of . . . Needless to say there were consequences to their disobedience. King Saul, the first Israeli king, was commanded to totally destroy the Amelikites, but he didn't. What were the consequences? God rejected him from being king, depriving his heirs from ever becoming kings.

Is God commanding you to do something? Remember, you do not have any choice in the matter. Obedience will bring blessings your way, and disobedience will most surely bring God's wrath.

When God counsels us, He allows us the freedom to choose, but cautions us to do whatever it is, His way. His counsel outlines the consequences of our choices so we know beforehand what to expect. He said to the Israelis, "I have set before you life and death, I counsel you to choose life." Similarly, He says in John 14: "I am the way, the truth, and the life; no man comes to the Father . . . People have the choice to choose life or death. If their choice leads to death, they will have no one but themselves to blame. Of course, God's counsel was for man to choose life. "Pray without ceasing" is a command, so is "love the Lord with all your heart" and many others. Are we obeying them?

GIVE GOD THE GLORY

"Apart from me you can do nothing." Jn 15:5

"I can do everything through Him who gives me strength." Php 4:13

When people are doing well, (all aspects) they turn to give the glory to everybody else including themselves except the One to whom it is really due, God. The glory should go to God because;

1) Jesus is at the right side of the Father interceding for us. Rom 8:34b, Heb 7:24-25 2) According to Scripture, the Spirit prays for us as well. Rom 8:26b

Our state of well—being therefore is not something we can take credit for, even when we do all the right things.

Existence

We are here because God wants us here; in other words we are not here by chance or by accident. He said to Jeremiah, "Before I formed you in the womb I knew you, before you were born I set you apart; I appointed you as a prophet to the nations." Jer 1:5

So we are here by divine appointment, for a purpose.

Understanding/ Insight into Spiritual things

Do you have any special abilities? They are gifts from the Holy Spirit; meant to be used to edify the Church, the body of Christ and for God's glory.

After Jesus' resurrection, He joined two disciples going from Jerusalem to Emmaus discussing the recent happenings. They were spiritually blind, and therefore could not tell it was Jesus who was walking with them. Finally at dinner, they recognized Him; only because Jesus opened their eyes. Lk 24:31

Later, He appeared to the eleven, and had to open their minds so they could understand the Scriptures regarding the prophecies concerning Him. Lk 24:45

Spiritual Well-being

Are you doing well in you walk with the Lord? Good, but don't take credit for it and don't boast about it. It's the Lord's doing. He has you covered. He is interceding for you. He said to Simon Peter, "Simon, Simon, Satan has asked to sift you as wheat. But I have prayed for you, Simon that your faith may not fail." Lk 22:31-32

If He is praying for us, why should we pray? Because He said so! Let's be obedient. We will understand it all someday when we see Him face to face.

Health and Healing

Doctors and the medical profession receive more recognition than God when health is restored. They should be commended for caring and working tirelessly.

But only God heals! "I am the Lord, who heals you." Ex 15:26b

God is the power behind all the scientific discoveries and technology that have greatly enhanced the delivery of healthcare. Also, He is the one who makes our bodies respond to whatever medicines we take and procedures we go through.

Wealth

Do you think your hard work has enabled you to have a good paying job, roof over your head, food on the table, money in the bank and a car in the driveway? Do you think you have attained the American dream; through your own efforts? Wrong attitude! Moses reminded the Israelites, "You may say to yourself, 'My power and the strength of my hands have provided this wealth for me.' But remember the Lord your God, for **it is He who** gives you the ability to produce wealth, and so confirms His covenant, which He swore to your forefathers, as it is today." Deut 8:17-18

Memorize—"What do you have that you did not receive? And if you did receive it, why do you boast as though you did not?" 1 Cor 4:7b

WHEN GOD MOVES HIS HAND

Sometimes things just don't go right, no matter what we do. No amount of prayers, personal or corporate, offered to God seem to make any difference. In fact situations most often get worse or remain unchanged.

We know God is touched by our pain, even though sometimes it seems He is on vacation, asleep or too busy with more important issues. "For we do not have a high priest who is unable to sympathize with our weaknesses," Heb 4:15 The devil on the other hand starts the trouble and looks for more ways to make it as unbearable as possible. He is determined to destroy us and our relationship with God.

The promises of God are such that one will think life should be smooth sailing for us. But not so! Instead, quite often, we run into unbelievable problems. I believe we run into problems when God removes His hand of protection and provision, making us vulnerable. Why would God do something like that, knowing the devil is out there like a roaring lion, waiting for the opportunity to pounce on us? 1 Pet 5:8

There are **at least** two reasons:

+ One, **God is confident** we can handle it, and wants to prove to the devil that we will go all the way with Him no matter what. Scary indeed! Remember Job? He was content to be a Godly man. He was not out to prove anything to anyone, but God was. God started that whole conversation with the devil about Job's integrity. Couldn't He have left it alone? All of a sudden, Job's world came crushing down, for no apparent reason. To make matters worse, the miserable comforters (ignorant friends) who went to supposedly sympathize with him only judged and criticized him, adding insult to injury.

+ Two, it could be, **there is sin in the camp!** Remember Achan? With God's help the walls of Jericho had collapsed, meaning a big victory for the Israelites. Ai, being a smaller city than Jericho was going to be undoubtedly a piece of cake for the Israelites to conquer, but to their surprise, they were literally chased out of town in disgrace. Why? Achan had sinned. (Jos 7) All of a sudden they no longer had Gods protection. In Isaiah 5, God likened the Israelites to a vineyard He had lovingly cared for, that yielded bad fruit. His response to that situation was, "I will take away its hedge, and it will be destroyed; I will break down its wall, and it will be trampled. I will make it a wasteland, neither pruned nor cultivated, and briers and thorns will grow there. I will command the clouds not to rain on it." Vs 5-6

I believe the only time the devil can touch us is when God removes His hand of protection. (Giving him permission) If God is out to prove something, we'll just have to go along with His program, trusting Him to sustain us through the experience. On the other hand, if it's because of sin in the camp, let's repent so we can be restored.

JOY COMES IN THE MORNING

"When the Lord brought back the captives to Zion, we were like men who dreamed. Our mouths were filled with laughter, our tongues with songs of joy. Then it was said among the nations, 'The Lord has done great things for them.' The Lord has done great things for us, and we are filled with joy." Ps 126:1-3

On the subject of trials, have you in hard times felt "the end will never come"? Have you ever felt a bad situation was like a nightmare, and you longed to wake up, and get back to real life?

Well, the Israelites knew that sort of thing very well. Captivity if I may say so was their middle name. For disobedience and idolatry, they were sent into captivity numerous times. During their struggles in captivity, they would cry out to the Lord. God loved them so much that each time, after He had taught them a lesson, He would bring them back to their own land.

This passage (Psalm 126:1-3) expresses their emotional state after one of their many captivity experiences.

They couldn't believe they were finally home. Their misery was over, they could laugh and sing. They probably needed someone to pinch them to assure them, they were really home, and that it was not a dream.

So in our trials, let us remember God is faithful and will bring deliverance, after we have mastered the lessons He is trying to teach us. "When you pass through the waters, I will be with you; and when you pass through the rivers, they will not sweep over you. When you walk through the fire, you will not be burned; the flames will not set you ablaze. For I am the Lord, your God, The Holy One of Israel, your Savior." Isaiah 43:2-3a

May God grant us patience to wait for the fulfillment of His promises. "For the revelation awaits an appointed time; it speaks of the end and will not prove false. **Though it linger, wait for it; it will certainly come and will not delay."** Hab 2:3

Then of course, we will bless the Lord for His mighty acts on our behalf. Observers will testify to what they have witnessed in our lives to the praise and glory of God. Until then, let us press on.

MEMORIZE **"Though it linger, wait for it, it will certainly come and will not delay."**
Hab 2:3b

BE HANNAH-LIKE

How would you feel if someone gave you something; only to take it back? Not very polite I'll say, but that's what we do often times with God. It is almost a routine for us to take our needs and concerns to God in prayer, and we should. The problem is, once we finish praying we take the burden back with us and continue to worry about it. Why do we do that?

Let's look at Hannah, Mrs Elkanah, Samuel's mother. She had a desperate need; she was barren (The Lord had closed her womb). All she wanted was one child, a son, to take away her reproach. To make matters worse, her rival, Peninnah who had children, taunted her mercilessly. It drove her to tears; often times she was so miserable she'd refused to eat. Her husband tried but could not comfort her. Finally, she took her need and misery to the Lord in prayer. As soon as she was done praying, according to the Scriptures, "She went her way and ate something, **and her face was no longer down-cast." 1 Sam 1:18b**

What a transformation! Hannah went from crying, being miserable and not eating, to, "no longer down-cast."

What was the reason for this quick turn around?

+ She knew who she had just prayed to-(God in Jesus' name.) "My Father will give you whatever you ask in my name." Jn 16:23b

+ She knew God's promises regarding asking and receiving. "Ask and it will be given to you; seek and you will find; knock and the door will opened to you. For everyone who asks receives; he who seeks finds; and to him who knocks, the door will be opened." Mt 7:7-8

+ She knew God's faithfulness. "If we are faithless, He will remain faithful, for He cannot disown Himself." 2 Tim 2:13 "Ask and you will receive, and your joy will be complete." Jn 16:24b

+ She knew God's view on anxiety. "Do not be anxious about anything, but in everything, by prayers and petition, with thanksgiving, present your requests to God. And the peace of God, which transcends all understanding, will guard your hearts and your minds in Christ Jesus." Php 4:6-7

+ She knew it was just a matter of time; **she was willing to wait.** "Those who hope (wait upon) in the Lord will renew their strength. They will run and not grow weary; they will walk and not faint." Isa 40:31

I need to be more Hannah-like, how about you? When we take our burden back we are in a way saying God cannot handle it, we can do a better job or we enjoy carrying that burden. From now on, let's drop our burden at His feet and leave it there.

BOOK REVISION

Webster defines revise as change or amend content of. With that in mind, I consider necessary the many revisions text books go through every few years to stay on the market. This process keeps the text current as new information becomes available. There are places that shy away from research based on text books that are five years or older, because of the fear that the information could be outdated.

That brings us to the Bible! Its contents will never be outdated! God is truth and He does not change. From everlasting to everlasting He is God. The Scriptures is God-breathed and is for all time. There will never be the need to revise the Bible, because His intentions and plans for mankind have never, and will never change.

We can study it as it is with the confidence that nothing in it is ever going to change. All we learn from it now will always be current. Therefore, we can and should apply its truths with reverence and obedience. Worldly truth changes so much; it used to be that people thought the world was flat. Many years later, based on discovery, the belief changed to the world being round. I won't be surprised if some other discovery in the near future suggests that the world is . . .

If Jesus is the word and He does not change then the word cannot change either. It stands true from generation to generation. We can put it to the test time after time and it will always prove true. This is very reassuring. For instance, 1 Jn 1:9 assures us of God's forgiveness and cleansing when we confess our sins. "If we confess our sins, He is faithful and just and **will** forgive us our sins and purify us from all unrighteousness." What condition would

we be in if that verse was revised to say, "He **might** forgive us."
What kind of assurance will there be in that? None!

There are unbelievers who think the Bible is an out-dated book. That way of thinking is what is robbing the world of absolute truth. People are creating their own truth. They want to do what seems right in their own eyes, and to add insult to injury, they want everyone else to say, "its okay." They don't want the Bible in the public school, government or public places; that's probably part of the reason why metal detectors are needed in all kinds of places including schools. We are sometimes labeled, old—fashion by people who so desperately want to make changes to the Bible to ease their conscience. Jesus clearly said, "Heaven and earth will pass away, but my words will never pass away." Lk 21:33

The song writer was right when he wrote about the Old Time Religion being good enough for him. "It was good enough for Paul and Silas; it's good enough for me." Again Jesus said, "Until heaven and earth disappear, not the smallest letter, not the least stroke of a pen, will by any means disappear from the law until everything is accomplished." Mt 5:18 God is able to protect it. After all, He has protected it for years and will continue to do so throughout eternity.

BRING OTHERS WITH YOU

I do not know of a single Christian who is not excited about going to heaven. We are eager, almost anxious to get there; to see Jesus face to face, and enjoy all the wonderful things He has promised us in His word. He's promised us streets of gold, pearly gates and mansions. There will be no need for light, because His presence will light up the place; there will be no more sickness, sadness, sorrow, tears, or death. There will be a great multitude of people from every tribe, tongue and nation. How awesome!

The thought of seeing God, face to face is quite exciting, but what will it be like for those who don't know Christ? They will go to a Christ-less eternity, in plain language, hell. The sad part of this is the fact that a lot of our friends and family are in this category. Don't we care? Shouldn't we care?

We get too caught up in our personal worlds; we don't put much effort into reaching the lost. Jesus came to save that which was lost. His goal and agenda for going to the cross was to save souls. He saved us and left us here so we can be a witness to those in our sphere of influence. How are we doing? The heart of God is missions. We don't have to go to a foreign country to do mission work. There are many unsaved people around us. They live in our neighborhoods, they work with us, we meet them in the gymnasium, the market places and everywhere else we go. Let's bring them with us to heaven. I think heaven will be a lot more exciting if our loved ones are there with us.

When people come to Christ, the number of people carrying out the great commission increases by that many and the work gets lighter. The faster we get the work done, the sooner our Lord will return. Let's be diligent. People die every day, but not all of them are saved. Sad to say, for the unsaved in this category, it is already too late. No amount of praying for the unsaved dead will build them a mansion in heaven, not even a hut (of course no huts in heaven, only mansions).

As long as people are alive, there is hope for them. However, that hope cannot be realized if we do not tell them the good news of Christ. It is our responsibility to make them aware; it is the Holy Spirit's responsibility to convict and save them. The Lord has not returned because He is giving the unsaved the opportunity to be saved, and giving us the opportunity to witness to them. "The Lord is not slow in keeping His promise, as some understand slowness. He is patient with you, not wanting anyone to perish, but everyone to come to repentance." 2 Pet 3:9 However, He is not going to wait forever.

Someday, on account of those we bring with us to heaven, may we hear the Lord say to us, "Well done, good and faithful servant! . . . Come and share your master's happiness" Mt 25:21 May we see many who made it to heaven because of our witness and testimony, and may we rejoice with all those who have cheered us on. What a reunion that will be!

GOD'S WRATH

Psalm 7:11 says, "God is angry with the wicked everyday"

ANGER strong feeling of displeasure (dictionary definition)
WRATH violent anger

"You alone are to be feared, **who can stand before you** when you are angry?" Ps 76:7

"How long O Lord? Will you **hide yourself forever?** How long will your wrath **burn like fire?**" Ps 89:46

". . . Though in anger I **struck you** . . . ." Isaiah 60:10

"See, the day of the Lord is coming, a cruel day, with wrath and fierce anger—**to make the land desolate and destroy the sinners within it."** Isaiah 12:9

"The wrath of God is being revealed from heaven against all the Godlessness and wickedness of men who suppress the truth by their wickedness." Rom. 1:18

THE UNBELIEVERS' RESPONSE

". . . They called to the mountains and the rocks, 'Fall on us and hide us from the face of Him who sits on the throne and from the wrath of the Lamb! For the great day of their wrath has come, and **who can stand?'"**
Rev. 6:16-17

OUR RESPONSIBILITY

"Knowing therefore the terror of the Lord, **we persuade men;**"
2 Cor 5:11

"I have seen these people," the Lord said to Moses . . . . "Now leave
me alone so that my anger may burn against them and that I may
destroy them . . ." **But Moses sought the favor of the Lord his
God.** "O Lord," he said, "Why should your anger burn . . . . , turn
from your fierce anger; relent and do not bring disaster on your
people" . . . **Then the Lord relented and did not bring on His
people the disaster He had threatened.**
Ex 32 :9-14

Remember God knew what He was going to do but He gave Moses
the opportunity to move His hand through prayer. We have the
same opportunity; let's use it to effect change.

LET HIM WHO HAVE NO SIN

Only God has the right to judge and condemn people; He has the right because He is sinless and is the one who laid down the laws. It is amazing that with all that power and right He is full of grace and mercy. He is patient with the sinner; repeatedly giving him the opportunity to repent. Our call is to correct, encourage and build up others in love.

Unfortunately, Christians fall short of these qualities (mercy and grace). We quickly look down on others who are not doing it our way. We judge and condemn, showing no mercy. God has shown us mercy; let's show it to others. The Christian's 'Holier than thou attitude', only drives people farther away from God. Like the Pharisees, we set our own standards and use that as a basis for condemning others. Let's stop making ourselves the measuring rod for others. The word of God should remain the only standard of measurement. Let's concentrate on measuring our own lives, and until we can honestly say we are perfect in every way, let's leave everybody else alone. If we all strive, individually, at measuring up to God's standards, showing mercy to everyone else when they fail, the world will be a better place.

I believe we can love people into the Kingdom. That is what God did with us. We should not condone sin but love the sinner. When the woman was caught in adultery, people were ready to stone her. Could someone have befriended her and help redirect her life? The irony is that she found favor and forgiveness with the only person who had the right to condemn her; those who should have shown compassion because they were sinners themselves, were the ones who picked up the stones, ready to throw. Yes, the Scripture condemns adultery but where is mercy? When Jesus forgave her, He also charged her to turn away from sin. "Then neither do I condemn you, go now and leave your life of sin." Jn 8:11

The only Individual who has the right to judge is usually so slow to judge. In fact He says (to the Pharisees), "You judge by human standards; I pass judgment on no one. But if I judge, my decisions are right, because I am not alone." Jn 8:15-16

So let's be slow to judge, and when we apply Scripture to situations, let's do it with love, mercy and kindness. Let's pray more and criticize less.

The next time you feel the edge to criticize or condemn another, ask yourself, "Am I perfect yet?" If we answer this question honestly, we most likely will become less critical of others. May God help us to cultivate a merciful spirit so we can love people even when they are clearly wrong. Let's leave judgment to God who will judge at the right time, because "There is only one Lawgiver and judge, the one who is able to save and destroy. But you—who are you to judge your neighbor?" Ja 4:12

MEMORIZE: "Do not judge, or you will be judged." Mt 7:1

IT IS URGENT

Our being here today does not guarantee our being here tomorrow. We could be very well today, but not so well tomorrow. We don't know what tomorrow holds; we don't know where we will be or what we will be doing. Although we know we might not be here tomorrow, it is still very easy to assume that we will be here. For that reason, we treat life with indifference; we move slowly about things and don't always do our very best. We allow opportunities to slip by as we think "O well, I will try again tomorrow." Tomorrow might not come; on the other hand it might come, but we might not be in it.

We treat life as if time belongs to us, or as if we can make time do whatever we want, and whenever we want. Prov 27: 1 reminds us, "Do not boast about tomorrow, for you do not know what a day may bring forth." James reminds us of the same thing, "Now listen, you who say, 'Today or tomorrow we will go to this or that city, spend a year there, . . .' What is your life? You are a mist that appears for a little while and then vanishes." Ja 4:13-14

The truth is time does not belong to us; it belongs to God. We have a deadline to meet, and when that time comes, be it sooner or later, we should have fulfilled our call with passion and diligence. That is why the Scripture says, "Whatever your hand finds to do, do it with all your might, for in the grave, where you are going, there is neither working nor planning nor knowledge nor wisdom." Ecc 9:10

When our allotted time to accomplish whatever is over, it Is over. All our intentions, hopes and desires come to a screeching halt. We cannot go back and redo, complete or undo. Having regrets won't change anything either. The end of the allotted time does not always mean death; poor health can put one in the same predicament. If we have talents, gifts and abilities that will benefit others and advance the cause of Christ, the time to use them is now. To be able to accomplish a call, we must first know what we have been called to do.

Knowing our call is just as urgent as fulfilling it. How can we try to fulfill a call we didn't even know we had? The first step is to pray to find out if we are overlooking our call, then pray for the ability, the zeal and joy to fulfill that call as long as it is called today.

The Lord of the talents is returning soon; He is going to demand some accountability. How are we going to respond? Would we be able to confidently say, "Master, you entrusted me with . . . See, I have gained so much more." Or are we going to say in shame, "I was afraid and went and hid your talent in the ground. See, here is what belongs to you." Mt 25:14-25 The time to use our gifts and talents is now. The time to fulfill our responsibilities is now, not tomorrow, and not next week. Tomorrow might be too late. Only God knows how much time we have, and since we are not privy to that information, we need to constantly be in the mode of urgency. Paul the apostle said at the end of his life, "I have fought a good fight, I have kept the faith. Now there is in store for me the crown of righteousness which the righteous Judge will award to me on that day-and not only to me, but also to all who have longed for his appearing." 2 Tim 4:7-8 What will be our declaration when we come to the end?

MISSED OPPORTUNITIES

It recently dawned on me in a very distinct way that the loss that comes with missed opportunities is very enormous. We each have only one life to live unless we happen to be Lazarus, and that one life goes by very fast. "The length of our days is seventy years, or eighty if we have the strength; yet their span is but trouble and sorrow, for they quickly pass, and we fly away." Ps 90:10

Starting with the unbeliever, the Bible says, "I tell you, now is the time of God's favor, now is the day of salvation." 2 Cor 6:2b Once the unbeliever misses the opportunity to get saved during his /her life time, the opportunity does not present itself again, not after death. It will be eternally too late for him/her to get saved.

To the believer, it is very clear that we've been saved to serve, and the Lord grants us opportunities to fulfill that responsibility. "For we are God's workmanship, created in Christ Jesus to do good works, which God prepared in advance for us to do." Eph 2:10

All the opportunities are designed with His glory in mind. So if we keep missing opportunity after opportunity, how do we expect to fulfill that responsibility? Occasionally, we get the opportunity back, but not often. For instance, if we miss an unbeliever's window of opportunity to get saved, he/she goes to a Christ-less eternity. Being remorseful about that lost opportunity does not change that person's destiny. If someone needs food today and we are unwilling or too busy to respond, tomorrow might be too late; we would have missed the opportunity to show God's love.

Since we don't have any guarantees about recovering missed opportunities, the wise king admonishes us, "Whatever your hand finds to do, do it with all your might, for in the grave, where you are going, there is neither working nor planning nor knowledge nor wisdom." Ecc 9:10 He also admonishes in Ecc 3:12 "I know that there is nothing better for men than to be happy and **do good** while they live."

If we take our charge seriously, we will have no regrets and have nothing to be ashamed of when we appear before the Lord. We will be able to say with the apostle Paul, excitedly, "I have fought the good fight, I have finished the race, I have kept the faith. Now there is in store for me the crown of righteousness, which the Lord, the righteous judge, will award to me on that day." 2 Tim 4:7-8 On the other hand if we don't take our charge seriously, God will use others to accomplish His purpose; we'll lose our reward. How would it feel to be in heaven with no rewards? I have no idea, but I want to be able to hear the Master say to me, "Well done, good and faithful servant! You have been faithful with a few things; I will put you in charge of many things. Come and share your Master's happiness!" Mt 25:21

MAKE AN OPENING IN THE ROOF!

Mark 2:1-5 records the healing of the paralytic. The paralytic had a health need, but did he ever consider asking for healing or did he choose to live with his condition? May be the physicians had not been able to help and he had given up hope of ever getting healed. Maybe he knew others in the same predicament who have not been healed. Mark doesn't say, so we'll never know.

However, hope was born when Jesus came to town. With such a large crowd, it seemed there was no way the paralytic man could get close to Jesus. As bleak as the situation seemed, the paralytic's healing was still possible. All he needed was the faith of a few caring friends. It appears the sick man's faith was not part of the equation at all. The four friends made an opening in the roof of the house where Jesus was, and then lowered him and his bed right in front of Jesus, by-passing all those in line outside the house and risking the destruction of another person's property.

Finally, he had the opportunity to be in Jesus' presence. "When Jesus saw THEIR FAITH He said to the paralytic, 'Son, your sins are forgiven.'" V 5a

Further down in verse 11, Jesus said to the paralytic, "I tell you, get up, take your mat and go home." So healing came to this man apparently without any effort on his part; it was the effort of others.

Do you know anyone who needs God's intervention?

Is the person asking God? If not, why not? Consider the following possible reasons.

Ignorance of what God can do

Ignorance of their situation and need
Has no personal relationship with God.
Too stressed to pray
Too sick to pray
Too discouraged and frustrated to pray
Etc.

There are family members, friends and neighbors who can benefit from this way of intervention.

Would you take it upon yourself, make an opening in the roof and let them down before Jesus? Those you pray for may or may not know you've wrestled in prayer on their behalf, but God will know, and you will be encouraged by the result.

According to the book of Job, after each season of feasting by Job's children, he would sacrifice a burnt offering on behalf of each child thinking, "Perhaps my children have sinned and cursed God in their hearts." Job 1:5b

Whether the children knew about this practice or not is not very relevant; God took note of Job's prayer and answered it accordingly.

Let's put our faith to work on each other's behalf. God does not contradict Himself.

CHRIST TO THE NATIONS

With the chaos and increasing evil we see around us, we are longing more and more for the Lord's return. However, we have work to do before His return. He is not willing for any to perish (2 Pet 3:9), and that is why He has committed to us the ministry of reconciliation (2 Cor 5:19). "Go ye therefore, and teach all nations . . . and, lo, I am with you always even unto the end of the world." Mt 28:19-20

HOW CAN WE SHARE CHRIST WITH THE WORLD AROUND US?

1. **LIVING GODLY LIVES—**

   "By this shall all men know that you are my disciples if you have love one to another." Jn 13:35

   "Ye are the light of the world. A city that is set on a hill cannot be hid. Neither do men light a candle, and put it under a bushel, but on a candlestick; and it gives light unto all that are in the house" Mt 5:14-15, Lk 11:33

   "Now then we are ambassadors for Christ." 2 Cor 5:20

2. **LOOKING FOR OPPORTUNITIES—**

   ". . . lift up your eyes, and look on the fields; for they are white already to harvest." Jn 4:35b

   "For a great door and effectual is opened unto me," 1 Cor 16:9

3. **SHARING VERBALLY—**

"How then shall they call on Him in whom they have not believed? And how shall they believe in Him of whom they have not heard? And how shall they hear without a preacher? Rom 10:14

4. **PRAYING**

"The harvest truly is plenteous, but the laborers are few; pray ye therefore the Lord of the harvest, that He will send forth laborers into His harvest." Mt 9:37-38

"Brethren, pray for us." 1 Thes 5:25

"Finally, brethren, pray for us that the word of the Lord may have free course, and be glorified . . ." 2 Thes 3:1

GRACE—PASS IT ON

You are so good, and can't stand those who are not like you
Before you boast about being good, feel irritated, judge or condemn
others, look back
Were you always that good?
Honestly, you weren't, but others tolerated you all the same
When they did, didn't it make life easier?
The times when they weren't so tolerable, didn't it feel awful?
Well then, do unto others as you would have them do unto you

You are so good, but didn't always use to be that way
Did you have power to make the change?
Did you just wish the change into happening?
If you could have changed on your own Christ would not have
died
You are different now because of God's grace
He forgave you through Christ, and is constantly transforming
you into his image
So you see, you are God's workmanship, in progress, through His
grace
By God's grace, you are what you are
So then, no room for, boasting or quick passage of judgment on
others
You have experienced God's grace, pass it on!

LET HEAVEN REJOICE

Whether we realize it or not, God wants to be a proud Father. He wants us to make Him proud. He wants to brag about us, He wants to rejoice over us, and He wants us to give Him reason to do that.

When on the highway, you don't have to look in too many directions before you find a car with a bumper sticker that expresses a parent's pride in their child's success or hard work. When children do well, parents are happy and proud; they will share their joy with anyone who will listen. God wants to do the same with us.

God was pleased with Abraham's faithfulness and obedience regarding Isaac, the heir of the promise. (Gen 22:1-18). Abraham did not hesitate to attempt to do exactly what God had asked of him, which was to sacrifice Isaac. Needless to say God was very proud of him. It is said of him, "Abraham believed God, and it was credited to him as righteousness." God was proud of Abraham!

God was pleased with David, the shepherd boy who became king over Israel, so much that he was referred to as "a man after God's own heart." In rebuking king Saul for his disobedience, and announcing his successor, Samuel said to him, "The Lord has sought out a man after His own heart and appointed him leader of His people, because you have not kept the Lord's command." 1 Sam 13:14b God was proud of David!

How about Job? God was so impressed with his walk; He said to Satan, "Have you considered my servant Job? There is no one on earth like him; he is blameless and upright, a man who fears God and shuns evil." Job 1:8 God was proud of Job!

What is God saying about you; what is He saying about me?

God knowing how obedient and faithful His Son will be in accomplishing His mission, on earth, said at His baptism, "This is my Son, whom I love; with Him I am well pleased." Mt 3:17b Need I say, God was proud of His Son?

At the end of Jesus' temptations in the wilderness, Scripture says, "The devil left Him, and angels came and attended Him." Mt 4;11 I can imagine the angels dancing and praising God for the victory Jesus won over the devil. God was proud!

In Luke 15:10, we learn that, "There is rejoicing in the presence of the angels of God over one sinner who repents." Let's get serious about soul winning so heaven can rejoice!

Like Jesus who used Scripture to defeat the devil, if we allow the word of God to rule our lives, we will be as victorious in our walk and heaven will rejoice. God will be proud!

Little children enjoy happy parents. They'll do anything to get their approval and make them happy. Let's aim at making God proud of us!

LET GOD BE THE JUDGE

We are all concerned about our image, and wonder, "What do they think of me?" Nobody likes to be misunderstood or misrepresented. We all like people to think well of us, and that is not such a bad thing as long as we understand that perceptions change from time to time and are not always accurate. One day it could be, "Hail to the Son of David." The next day could be, "Crucify Him."

The reason peoples' perception of us could be distorted is that they don't have all the facts, and they misinterpret the little bit they have, making their conclusions biased and inaccurate. It's like doing a research with insufficient data. So if we want an honest opinion, there's only one dependable source to go to—God. He is all knowing, all seeing and understands it all. He knows our hearts, motives and our circumstances. He knows the reasons behind the things we do. He has all the data on which to base our Report Card.

God said to the Church of Sardis in Revelation 3:1b, "You have a reputation of being alive, but you are dead." How shocking! Everybody in town thought the Church was alive. I wonder what 'Alive' meant to them. The difference between the two reports is like the difference between night and day. Was the Church of Sardis all puffed up because of the reputation of being alive? Maybe! But was it really alive? God said NO, It was dead! He warned, "Wake up! Strengthen what remains and is about to die, for I have not found your deeds complete in the sight of my God." V2

We are not only concerned about what others think of us; we also like to think highly of ourselves. More often than not, we are just as wrong in our self-assessment as others are of us. To the Church in Laodicea, God said, "You say 'I am rich; I have acquired wealth and do not need a thing. But you do not realize that you are wretched, pitiful, poor, blind and naked." Rev 4:17 Again, God's assessment was totally different from the Church's assessment of itself.

Why is it that we are so interested in hearing nice things said about us? Shouldn't we also try to find out our failures so we can correct them? We seem to have excuses when our failures come up. We get defensive, feel insulted and belittled. Proverbs reminds us. "Wounds from a friend can be trusted." Prov 27:6a

When God tells it like it is, He also offers grace and mercy so we can make the needed corrections. His intentions for confronting us with our failures is not to put us down, but rather to build us up and make us fit for the Master's use.

Any time we want to really have an opinion of ourselves, let's ask God. He will tell us through His word. There will be no guess work or assumptions, just the truth. "Let God be true, and every man a liar." Rom 3:4b

Memorize: "Anyone who listens to the word but does not do what it says is like a man who looks at his face in a mirror and, immediately forgets what he looks like." Ja 1:23-24

HINDRANCES TO PRAYER

SIN "If I had cherished sin in my heart, the Lord would not have listened." Ps 66:18
(Also read Isaiah 1:10-20)
"Surely the arm of the Lord is not too short to save, but your iniquities have separated
you from your God, your sins have hidden His face from you, so that He will not hear."
Isaiah 59:1-2
"Then they will cry out to the Lord, but He will not answer them. At that time He will hide His face from them because of the evil they have done." Micah 3:4

Disobedience "He inquired of the Lord, but the Lord did not answer him . . ." 1 Sam 28:6
(Saul had disobeyed God prior to this verse)
"When I called they did not listen, so when they called I would not listen." Zec 7:13

Indifference "But since you rejected me when I called and no one gave heed when I stretched out my hand, since you ignored all my advice and would not accept my rebuke, I in turn will mock when calamity overtakes you . . . Then they will call to me but I will not answer" Prov 1:24-28

Neglect of Mercy "If a man shuts his ears to the cry of the poor, he too will cry out and not be answered" Prov 21:13

Despising the law "If anyone turns a deaf ear to the law, even his prayers are detestable." Prov 28:9

The devil's interception "Do not be afraid . . . I have come in response to them. But the prince of the Persian kingdom resisted me twenty-one days" Dan 10:12-13

Instability in faith "But when he asks, he must believe and not doubt . . . that man should not think he will receive anything from the Lord." James 1:6-7

Motives "When you ask, you do not receive, because you ask with wrong motives . . . ." James 4:3

Individually, let us daily, take stock of our lives making sure we know of nothing that will hinder our prayers. We cannot afford hindered prayers.

PRAYER

When do you pray? May be:

1. When you have a need
2. when you feel like it
3. when it is convenient
4. when you have nothing else to do

Prayer sometimes has to be instantaneous, as a need arises or as we feel thankful etc.

Aside from the instantaneous times, we need to make time for daily prayers. How many people expect their children to talk to them only when they feel like it, or when it is convenient for them? Our heavenly Father expects no less. Even when we cannot identify a need to pray about, let us go into His presence to worship, meditate, fellowship and listen.

Jesus made time to communicate with His Father.

"Very early in the morning, while it was still dark, Jesus got up, left the house and went off to a solitary place, where He prayed." **Mk 1:35.**

"And when He had sent them away, He departed into a mountain to pray." **Mk 6:46.**

"And He withdrew Himself into the wilderness and prayed." **Lk 5:16**

If we wait till it's convenient, we will pray very little or not at all. We have to purpose in our hearts to **pray DAILY**, and make it a priority. In other words, prayer should be on the list of things we do every day. Other items on our lists may change from day to day, but **PRAYER** is one of the items that should never change. Prayer is our way of communicating with the Father, and also weapon against the unseen powers, "For our struggle is not against flesh and blood, but against the rulers, against the authorities, against the powers of this dark world and against the spiritual forces of evil in the heavenly places." **Eph 6:12**

OUR ADMONITION

"Pray in the spirit on all occasions with all kinds of prayers and requests. With this in mind, be alert and always keep on praying for all the saints." **Eph 6:18**

"Pray continually (without ceasing) . . . . for this is God's will for you in Christ Jesus." **1Thes 5: 17-18**

"But when you pray, go into your room, close the door and pray to your Father, who is unseen. Then your Father, who sees what is done in secret, will reward you." **Mt 6:6**

MEMORIZE **"Pray without ceasing, give thanks in all circumstances, for this is God's will for you in Christ Jesus." 1 Thes 5: 17-18**

PRAY FOR ME / I WILL PRAY FOR YOU

Have you ever asked someone to pray for you? Have you ever agreed or offered to pray for another person? That is what we are called to do as brothers and sisters, to pray for each other because "The prayer of a righteous man is powerful and effective." Ja 5:16b

The Apostle Paul was a man of prayer. He never ceased to pray for the saints and for the churches. He always thanked God at the remembrance of them. Phil 1:3-4, Eph 1:15-16 He prayed that the churches will be equipped to be effective in ministry.

He prayed specifically for their growth. For example, in Ephesians 1:17, "I keep asking that the God of our Lord Jesus Christ, the glorious Father, may give you the Spirit of wisdom and revelation, so that you may know him better. I pray also that the eyes of your heart may be enlightened in order that you may know the hope to which He has called you." Eph 1:17-18a

In Philippians 1:9-10, he told them, "And this is my prayer: that your love may abound more and more in knowledge and depth of insight, so that you may be able to discern what is best and may be pure and blameless until the day of Christ."

As prayerful a man as Paul was, you would think he could pray enough for himself, and I'm sure he did, but he also coveted the prayers of other believers. He never thought of himself as a self-sufficient spiritual giant; instead, he said to the Thessalonians, "Brothers, pray for us." 1 Th 5:25

"Finally, brothers, pray for us that the message of the Lord may spread rapidly." 2 Th 3:1

"Pray also for me, that whenever I open my mouth, words may be given me so that I will fearlessly make known the mystery of

the gospel . . . . Pray that I may declare it fearlessly, as I should."
Eph 6:19-20

"And pray for us, too, that God may open a door for our message, so that we may proclaim the mystery of Christ . . . Pray that I may proclaim it clearly, as I should." Col 4:3-4

We need to remember to pray for each other whether asked or not. But when asked, or when we offer to pray, let's not forget to actually pray. Wishing and hoping are not enough. There is no point in giving people false hope and assurances. Also, let's follow up with each other to see how these prayers are being answered so that we can give thanks to God for His faithfulness. Psalm 107 teaches us to praise and thank the Lord for what He does for us. Recounting what God has done reminds us that we serve a great God and encourages us to continue to trust Him.

PRAYING FOR THE SAINTS

Praying for the saints is not a suggestion; it is a command that we need to obey like all other commands. "... be alert and always keep on praying for all the saints." Eph 6:18b God commands that for a good reason. He never asks us to do anything for no reason. He knows what we need, and He knows the avenue through which He will provide them, and apparently, it is through prayer. So if He commands us to pray, we need to pray without asking questions. But for what should we pray? The Bible actually tells us the areas we need to focus our prayers on when praying for each other. Let's look at some of those ideas:

To Encourage—It is encouraging to know that we are being prayed for; hence like the apostle Paul, we need to let others know we are praying for them. In Romans 1: 9-10a, Paul says, "God, whom I serve with my whole heart in preaching the gospel of his Son, is my witness how constantly I remember you in my prayers at all times." "We continually remember before our God and Father your work produced by faith, your labor prompted by love, and your endurance inspired by hope in our Lord Jesus Christ." 1 Th 1:3 "... since the day we heard about you, we have not stopped praying for you and asking God to fill you with the knowledge of His will through all spiritual wisdom and understanding. And we pray this in order that you may live a life worthy of the Lord and may please Him in every way ... in the kingdom of light." Col 1:9-12 "I want you to know how much I am struggling for you ... My purpose is that they may be encouraged in heart and united in love ... know the Mystery of God, namely Christ, in whom are hidden all the treasures of wisdom and knowledge." Col 2:1-3

Thanksgiving (to God)—we need to be thankful as we see God use others, as we see growth and maturity in each other's lives, and as we see prayers for each other answered. "I always thank God for you because of His grace given you in Christ Jesus . . . God who has called you into fellowship with his Son Jesus Christ our Lord, is faithful." 1 Cor 1:4-9 "I thank my God every time I remember you. In all my prayers for all of you, I always pray with joy because of your partnership in the gospel." Php 1:3-5a "We always thank God, the Father of our Lord Jesus Christ, when we pray for you, because we have heard of your faith in Christ Jesus and of the love you have for all the saints." Col 1:3-4 "I always thank my God as I remember you in my prayers, because I hear about your faith in the Lord Jesus and your love for all the saints." Philemon 1:4-5 ". . . we constantly pray for you, that our God may count you worthy of His calling, and that by His power He may fulfill every good purpose of yours and every act prompted by your faith. We pray this so that the name of our Lord Jesus may be glorified in you." 2 Th 1:11-12a

Manifestation of the power of the Spirit-
"I pray that out of His glorious riches He may strengthen you with power through His Spirit in your inner being, so that Christ may dwell in your hearts through faith. And I pray that you, being rooted and established in love may have power . . . that you may be filled to the measure of all fullness of God." Eph 3:14-19 ". . . we constantly pray for you, that our God may count you worthy of His calling, and that by His power he may fulfill every good purpose of yours and every act prompted by your faith." 2 Th 1:11

Better Knowledge of God—"I keep asking . . . may give you the Spirit of wisdom and revelation, so that you may know Him better. I pray also that the eyes of your heart may be enlightened in order that you may know the hope to which He has called you." Eph 1:17-18 ". . . we have not stopped praying for you and asking God to fill you with the knowledge of His will through all spiritual wisdom and understanding." Col 1:9

Spiritual Growth—And this is my prayer: that your love may abound more and more in knowledge and depth of insight, so that you may be able to discern what is best and may be pure and blameless until the day of Christ, filled with the fruit of righteousness that comes through Jesus Christ-to the glory and praise of God." Php 1:9-11

Evangelism—"I pray that you may be active in sharing your faith, so that you will have a full understanding of every good thing we have in Christ." Philemon 1:6

PSALM 15

"Lord, who may dwell in your sanctuary? Who may live on your holy hill?

He whose walk is blameless and who does what is righteous, who speaks the truth from his heart and has no slander on his tongue, who does his neighbor no wrong and casts no slur on his fellowman, who despises a vile man but honors those who fear the Lord, who keeps his oath even when it hurts, who lends his money without usury and does not accept a bribe against the innocent. He who does these things will never be moved."

QUESTION

Who may dwell in your sanctuary? Who may dwell in your holy hill?

In short, who may come into your presence, who may seek fellowship with you?

ANSWER

He whose walk is blameless and who does what is righteous

AS CHRISTIANS, HOW CAN OUR WALK BE BLAMELESS?

1. Speak the truth from the heart (avoid pretences, exaggerations, intentional misleading and omissions; it is better to not address an issue than lie about it. God knows your heart)
2. No slander (avoid false, defamatory spoken statements)

3. Do your neighbor no wrong (your neighbor is anybody you encounter who is not you)
4. Cast no slur on your fellowman (do not belittle others)
5. Regard a vile person for what he is (do not throw in your lot with evil people, avoid them if you have to)
6. Honor those who fear the Lord (whoever loves and fears your Lord, hold in high esteem)
7. Keep your promises no matter what. (So make promises wisely)
8. Lend without charging interest (unless you are a bank of course)
9. Do not accept a bribe against the innocent (do not allow yourself to be coerced or bribed into giving false testimonies)

LET US CONTINUE TO PRAY FOR EACH OTHER, "for our struggle is not against flesh and blood, but against the rulers, against the authorities, against the powers of this dark world and against the spiritual forces of evil in the heavenly realms." Eph 6:12

PSALM 23

Are you a sheep? Would you like to be safe?
Then you need a Shepherd!
The Shepherd has other sheep
To be under His watchful eyes, you need to stay in the fold
The Shepherd has only one fold

Are you a sheep?
The devil has his eyes on you
Like a roaring lion, he seeks to devour you
You wonder away from the fold at your own risk
The lion is lurking,
Hoping to pounce on you at your unguarded moment

Are you a sheep?
Stay prayerfully in the fold
Listen to the Shepherd's voice
Follow the Shepherd's leading
Seek the prayer-covering of fold mates
Then you'll know and enjoy the Shepherd's protection

LESSONS FROM RAHAB JOSHUA 2:1-21

After the death of Moses, Joshua was charged with leading the Israelites into the Promised Land. Joshua sent two men to go and spy out Jericho. In Jericho, the Bible says the men entered a house belonging to Rahab, a harlot.

1. Why did the spies go to Rahab's house and not to another? God is in control of our lives and circumstances. Nothing happens to us by chance. "Are not two sparrows . . . yet not one of them will fall to the ground apart from the will of your Father." Mt 10:29

2. How many people will trust a harlot with anything important? Harlots have very poor reputation, making it easy for the average person to discount them, but God didn't discount Rahab, God is no respecter of persons. Rom 2:11 In addition, Rahab, the harlot was an ancestor of Jesus Christ. Mt 1:1-5

3. Rahab put her life on the line when she hid the spies, and made up a cover-up story. We have the responsibility to protect those who can't protect themselves. Corrie ten Boom helped many Jews escape the Nazis during World War II. "Rescue the weak and needy; deliver them from the hand of the wicked." Ps 82:4

   When the king heard about Rahab's visitors, he demanded that they be turned over to him. She lied to protect them. V 2-6

4. Is God advocating lying? By no means! The Bible is just stating the facts of the case. If she hadn't lied, God would still have found a way of protecting the spies.

5. Rahab reported to the spies that the people of Jericho had been panicking on account of the Israelites. V 10-11 Does your life or what people hear about you challenge them, or do they never want to be Christians? "Let your life so shine before men that they may see your good works . . ." Mt 5:16

6. In exchange for protecting the spies, Rahab requested protection for herself and her family when Jericho was attacked. V12-13 We need to pray for the salvation of others. The apostle Paul prayed for the Jews, "Brothers, my heart's desire and prayer to God for the Israelites is that they may be saved." Rom 10:1

7. The spies responded to Rahab's request by laying down the ground rules by which her request would be honored. She would have to tie the red cord in the window, a reminder that her house should not be attacked. V 17-19 The blood of Christ is the sign that we are forgiven. We have passed from death to life. Jn 5:24b "When I see the blood, I will pass over you." Ex 12:13. The Holy Spirit is our guarantee for the future. 2 Cor 1:22b

8. To ensure their safety, Rahab was charged with bringing her family into her house. If anyone wondered outside, they would lose their guaranteed protection. V18-19 Christians need to be in each other's company to encourage one another. Spending time together and praying for and with each other, have protective properties. Stay in the fold and be protected. "Your enemy the devil prowls around like a roaring lion looking for someone to devour." 1Pet 5:8

READING THE WORD WITH UNDERSTANDING

The Bible is the inspired word of God. "Above all, you must understand that no prophecy of Scripture came about by the prophet's own interpretation. For prophecy never had its origin in the will of man, but **men spoke from God** as they were carried along by the Holy Spirit." 2 Peter 2:20-21 Again it says, "All Scripture is **God-breathed** and useful for teaching, rebuking, correcting and training in righteousness, so that the man of God may be thoroughly equipped for every good work." 2 Tim 3:16

How useful can it be if we do not understand it? Therefore, we need the Holy Spirit's guidance whenever we read the Bible. Let's be thankful that we are educated, and therefore able to read, but that does not guarantee our understanding. The Ethiopian eunuch could read but had no understanding of what he was reading. Acts 8:26-31

Before Christ's ascension, He appeared to His disciples; He reinforced what He had told them in the past concerning the purpose of His death. During that encounter, Scripture says, "Then He opened their minds so they could understand the Scriptures." Lk 24:45 They would not have understood otherwise, had He not opened their minds.

Unbelievers cannot understand or interpret the Scriptures because they do not have the Spirit of God. However, we can, because the Spirit of truth dwells within us and will teach us all things if we allow ourselves to be taught. Like the Psalmist, we need to approach the bible prayerfully; he prayed, "Open my eyes that I may see wonderful things in your law." Ps 119:18 So the Psalmist understands that if the Spirit does not illumine his spiritual eyes, no amount of reading could bring understanding, and he would miss out on wonderful things in the word.

Unless we understand what we read, we cannot trust it, obey it or share it.

We are commanded to be doers of the word, (Ja 1:22) but how can we if we do not understand it.

The Psalmist had a lot to say about the benefits of the word of God. He had proved it to be true and faithful. Numerous times in the Scriptures, he expresses his thoughts about the word of God. In Psalm 119, he states it in many different ways, "How sweet are your words to my taste." Ps 119:103 In order to be that excited about the word, we need to understand its message.

"The unfolding of your word gives light." Ps 119:130 Unless the word is unfolded, (opened and spread out) it cannot benefit us, because when it remains folded its message is hidden, and we cannot gain understanding, wisdom, or light for our path. "Thy word is a lamp to my feet and a light for my path." Ps 119:105

How then can we understand the word of God? By reading it prayerfully, meditating on it and allowing the Spirit to speak to our hearts. Ask other believers to see if they have a better understanding. There is nothing shameful about asking. We are here to support and encourage each other.

So the next time you read your Bible, hopefully soon, read it prayerfully, trusting the Spirit to help you understand.

SEEKING GOD

"If my people, which are called by my name, shall humble themselves and pray, and **seek my face**, and turn from their wicked ways; then will I hear from heaven, and will forgive their sin, and will heal their land." 2 Ch 7:14

How Do we SEEK God?

SEEK—search for (dictionary definition)
SEEKING GOD—A diligent search to find Him, know Him, learn of Him, walk with Him, depend on Him, trust and obey Him. (Pearl's definition)

Seeking God involves the will. One must want to, desire to, decide to, and take steps to find Him. "Those from every tribe of Israel who set their hearts on seeking the Lord, the God of Israel, followed the Levites to Jerusalem to offer sacrifices to the Lord, the God of their fathers." 2 Ch 11:16

FINDING GOD'S WILL AND OBEYING IT

Where do we find His will? Read the Bible diligently. "I have hidden your word in my heart that I might not sin against you." Ps 119:11

"He did not consult the Baals but sought the God of his father and followed His commands rather the practices of Israel." 2 Ch 17:3b-4

"I seek you with all my heart; do not let me stray from your commands." Ps 119:10

SEEKING GOD THROUGH PRAYER

<u>Confess and denounce sin</u>
"Wash away all my iniquity and cleanse me from my sin. For I know my transgressions, and my sin is always before me." Ps 51:2-3
"I prayed to the Lord my God and confessed:" Dan 9:4

<u>Desiring His will</u>
"In the course of time, David inquired of the Lord, 'shall I go up to one of the towns of Judah?" The Lord said, go up." 2 Sam2:1
"And the Israelites inquired of the Lord." Judges 20:27

<u>Showing Dependence on Him</u>
"Whenever God slew them, they would seek Him." Ps 78:34
"They were helped in fighting them, because they trusted in Him." 1 Ch 5:20
". . . they were being attacked . . . Then they cried out to the Lord." 2 Ch 13:14
". . . Asa called to the Lord, the Lord struck down the Cushites before Asa." 2 Ch 14:11-12
"Hear my cry O God, listen to my prayer." Ps 61:1
"I am only a little child . . . give your servant a discerning heart to govern . . ." 1 King 3:7-9

SEEKING GOD THROUGH FELLOWSHIP WITH OTHER BELIEVERS

"Then those who feared the Lord talked with each other, and the Lord listened and heard." Malachi 3:16

"Let us not give up meeting together as some are in the habit of doing, but let us encourage one another." Heb 10:25

RESULTS OF SEEKING GOD

"If you seek Him, He will be found by you." 1 Ch 28:9b

"As long as he sought the Lord God gave him success." 2 Ch 26:5b

"You will seek me and find me when you seek me with all your heart." Jer 29:13

Sin

Sin is defined in 1 Jn 3:4b as lawlessness and in 1 Jn 5:17 as all wrong doing. Christians are not immune to sin. We are guilty of both sins of omission and commission. We sin quite often in thought, deed and word. We also sin by leaving undone what we've been commanded to do. To help us maintain a healthy relationship and unbroken fellowship with God, He has given us His Spirit who convicts us so we will repent, be forgiven and restored.

Sin puts a separation between us and God. "Surely the arm of the Lord is not too short to save, nor His ear dull to hear. But your iniquities have separated you from your God; your sins have hidden His face from you, so that He will not hear." Isa 59:1-2

Sin interrupts our fellowship with God, until we confess and are forgiven. God sees everything we do; we cannot sweep anything under the carpet. God does not make excuses for anybody's sins. (Moses was punished, David was punished) He will judge sin wherever and whenever He finds it. Many times human parents overlook their children's wrongdoing, because they are too tired or don't want to be bothered. Not so with God, He defines sin the same way every time. Whatever is punishable today is punishable tomorrow and always. He is a consistent God. He does not frown upon something one day, ignore it the next day and smile at it another time. The consequences of sin are the same every time. The Psalmist says, "If I had cherished sin in my heart the Lord would not have listened." Ps 66:18

Do you wonder why your prayers seem to bounce off the ceiling sometimes? Although unanswered prayers are not always the result of sin, it is always a good time for us to examine our hearts to see if we are overlooking something. The Israelites defeated Jericho without a single 'shot.' They went against Ai, a smaller city, which should have been a piece of cake, but instead, they were miserably defeated. Why? There was sin in the Israelite camp! Achan had stolen and hidden stuff he was supposed to leave alone. Joshua and the leaders, broken-hearted, went to God in prayer. God's response was, "Israel has sinned . . . I will not be among you anymore unless you destroy whatever among you is devoted to destruction." Josh 7:11-12

Sin is sin, no matter what fancy name you give it. Society is working hard to get Christians to accept as okay things that God has said are not okay. The Christian is branded as intolerable if he or she does not go along with society's way of thinking. Who is right, God or society? In Isa 5:20, God says to the people, "Woe to those who call evil good and good evil, who put darkness for light and light for darkness, who put bitter for sweet and sweet for bitter."

When are we going to start weeping seriously over sin? Even though we should not tolerate sin, we need to show love and mercy to whoever is committing it, remembering that we are no better except that we have been saved by grace. We need to be firm in our stand against sin; but be kind in our attitude. Regarding the woman caught in adultery, Jesus said to the Pharisees, "If any one of you is without sin, let him be the first to throw a stone at her." Jn 8:7b

STANDING IN THE GAP

God is looking for people to stand in the gap. In other words, God is looking for intercessors. God hates sin and must punish it regardless of who commits it, the Christian as well as the unbeliever. Yet out of His love for man, He is always looking for ways and reasons to pardon and show mercy. He wants prayers to move Him to forgive.

In Ezekiel 22, God enumerated Jerusalem's sins, and as His holiness required, He must judge them. However, He wished He didn't have to, and longed for somebody to intercede for them, to turn His wrath away, **but there was nobody**. In verses 30-31, He says to Ezekiel, "I looked for a man among them who would build up the wall and stand before me in the gap on behalf of the land so I would not have to destroy it, **but I found none**. So I will pour out my wrath on them and consume them with my fierce anger, bringing down on their own heads all they have done, declares the Sovereign Lord."

There is sin around us at every turn, both in the church and outside the church. Are we concerned in any way? Then let's stand in the gap. We need to weep over the issues, child molestation, abuse, murder, rape, and all forms of violence. Let's stop the long discussions; instead, let's pray. God is looking for someone to stand in the gap and intercede for family, friends, neighbors, the unsaved and government. Let's not forget the poor and the needy as well. Jesus has already paid the price for sin; now God is looking for someone to pray for the sinner to come to salvation in Christ. He is also looking for someone to pray for the backslider and the prodigal to come back home.

Moses stood in the gap numerous times for the Israelites. When they made the golden calf in the wilderness, God was terribly displeased with them. Moses prayer was, "Oh, what a great sin these people have committed! They have made themselves gods of gold. But now, **please forgive their sin,** but if not, then blot me out of the book you have written." Ex 32: 31-32

He was even willing to lose his relationship with God if He wouldn't forgive.

Also, Moses interceded specifically for Aaron who made the golden calf, for God had wanted to destroy him, "But at that time I prayed for Aaron too." Deut 9:20 God even said to Moses in those days, "Let me alone, so that I may destroy them and blot out their name from under heaven." Deut 9:14a

However, Moses' prayer stayed God's hands!

When Daniel learned from the Scriptures how long the desolation of Jerusalem was going to be, he quickly took it upon himself to stand in the gap. He prayed confessing his sins and that of his people. Dan 9

When Ezra heard about the ungodly practices going on Israel, regarding marriage, he went into mourning and prayer, "O my God, I am too ashamed and disgraced to lift up my face to you, my God, because our sins are higher than our heads and our guilt has reached to the heavens. From the days of our forefathers until now, our guilt has been great. Because of our sins, we and our kings and our priests have been subjected to the sword and captivity, to pillage and humiliation at the hand of foreign kings, as it is today." Ezra 9:6—7

God is still looking for someone to stand in the gap. Do you know anyone for whom you can stand in the gap? Please do, because the prayer of a righteous man is powerful and effective. James 5:16b

Those we intercede for may never know, but God will honor our faithfulness and do what we request on behalf of others, for His glory.

RESOURCES FOR SURVIVAL AND GROWTH

We need the right resources in our walk as Christians in order to survive and grow. After conversion, Christians generally get to stay in the world. God does not usually remove us from it. He needs us to stay and be His hands, feet, eyes and mouth pieces. Even though we are in the world, we are no longer of the world. Now we are of Christ. In order to survive in the world and not be overwhelmed by it, and be able to grow more into Christ's likeness, we need to efficiently put our resources to use.

+ **The word (the Bible)**—The word of God is our map, lamp and guide as we journey through this life. It instructs us, directs us and teaches us how to apply the word to our lives so we can grow in our relationship with the Lord, avoid the pitfalls along the way and also avoid being sucked back into the world. In other words, it enables us to walk and live victoriously for the Lord, and in the end arrive in heaven. "Your word is a lamp to my feet and a light for my path." Ps 119:105 Concerning God's commands, the Proverbs say, "Bind them upon your heart forever; fasten them around your neck. When you walk, they will guide you; when you sleep, they will watch over you; when you wake, they will speak to you. For these commands are a lamp, this teaching is a light." Prov 6:21-23 "I have hidden your word in my heart that I might not sin against you." Ps 119:11

+ **Prayer**—Let us take a quick look at children. They have such a need to communicate with their parents. From the beginning, they communicate with their eyes, smile, cry and coos. Once they learn to actually talk, they engage parents in all kinds of conversations. They discuss everything they feel or think, they ask questions about whatever they do not understand. Through that process, they gain understanding, feel loved and appreciated. We need to relate to God in that same way. Unlike human parents, God never tires of hearing us. We will never hear Him say, "Child, I am tired" or "I need to go to work" or "I need to take this phone call" or "Tell me tomorrow." He is available to us 24/7. "What other nation is so great as to have their gods near them the way the Lord our God is <u>near us whenever we pray to Him</u>?" Deut 4:7 "The Lord detests the sacrifice of the wicked, but <u>the prayer of the upright</u> pleases Him." Prov 15:8 "Then Jesus told His disciples a parable to show them that <u>they should always pray and not give up</u>." Lk 18:1

- **Holy Spirit**—We need the Holy Spirit to comfort us, teach us, prompt us, convict us and pray through us. "But the Counselor, the Holy Spirit, whom the Father will send in my name, will teach you all things and will remind you of everything I have said." Jn 14:26 "In the same way, the Spirit helps us in our weakness . . . the Spirit Himself intercedes for us with groans that words cannot express." Rom 8:26

- **Christian Fellowship**—We are brothers and sisters walking the same path. Our struggles are not unique; they are common to each one of us. "No temptation has seized you, except what is common to man." 1 Cor 10:13 We need to share our problems and victories to encourage one another. We need to come together, routinely, in worship, in breaking bread, in prayer and study of the word. We need to pray for one another and enjoy one another's company. "Let us not give up meeting together, as some are in the habit of doing, but let us encourage one another." Heb 10:25

TAKING SIN LIGHTLY

"Can a man scoop fire into his lap without his clothes being burned? Can a man walk on hot coals without his feet being scorched?" Prov 6:27-28

God hates sin because He is holy. He cannot co-exist with sin. For that reason He wants us to hate it as well. He has given us the Holy Spirit, and one of His responsibilities is to prompt us when sin is close or convict us when we fall into sin.

Sin always has consequences! God is no respecter of persons, and He does not play favoritism when it comes to punishing sin. Nevertheless, we sometimes act as if there will be no consequences for the wrong we do. We explain it away, only deceiving ourselves and our listeners. God cannot be deceived or talked into thinking lightly of our sins.

Like the illustration in Proverbs 6:27-28, consequences are the natural, spontaneous results of sin. For example, Sampson knew the secret of his strength, he was a Nazirite; set apart for God. So why did he entertain Delilah's constant torment about revealing the source of his strength? She tried everything he told her, tying him with seven fresh thongs, tying him with new ropes, weaving the braids of his head into the fabric and tightening it with a pin and finally shaving him bald. One would think since she tried everything she was told; Sampson would have realized she most likely would shave off his hair as well, but he told her the truth anyway because he got tired of her naggings. As a result, he lost the strength and was captured by the Philistines who gouged out his eyes. (Judges 16) If God says, "Don't shave your hair," He means, don't shave you hair.

David, the king of Israel knew better, but being consumed with lust, he committed adultery with Bathsheba, and had her husband murdered. God did not look the other way or cover this sin. Although David was a man after His own heart, He exposed his sin and judged it. (2 Sam 11-12)

Solomon, the wisest man to ever walk the face of the earth fell into the same predicament for ignoring God's commands to the Israelites. The commands were for every one of them with no exception, be it king or servant. "Do not marry foreign women!" But Solomon, with all that wisdom still disobeyed. He could have had any Israeli virgin he wanted; all he had to do as king was say the word and any number of women could have been his. Unfortunately, he chose to marry foreign women and as he aged; they turned his heart after idols so that he was no longer fully devoted to God. How sad! Needless to say God judged him. (1 Kings 11)

These stories are for our learning. "All Scripture is God-breathed and is useful for teaching, rebuking, correcting and training in righteousness, so that the man of God may be thoroughly equipped for every good work." 2 Tim 3:16-17 Sin has consequences!

TASTE AND SEE

It is easy for us to want to try products and services based on commercials we see on TV, billboards; in magazines or in newspapers, or based on another person's testimony. We feel we owe it to each other to share the experiences we've had with products and services, whether good or bad. I am thinking of experiences like: good places to dine, to shop, to vacation, etc. We also compare notes about companies with good services and or prices. On many occasions, we've purchased things, visited restaurants or used certain merchants based on the recommendations of others. How about choosing a doctor or hospital? We all like to go to doctors recommended by others. Nobody would like to go to a doctor who has a reputation of being rude or having poor bedside manners. How many people will knowingly go to dine at a bug-infested restaurant? Making recommendations imply that we are one hundred percent convinced about a service, product or something. Personal experiences are very difficult to dispute, and because of that, businesses do from time to time request to be recommended to others by their existing clients.

This analogy applies in the Spiritual world as well. Jesus says of Himself "I am the bread of life. He who comes to me will never go hungry, and he who believes in me will never be thirsty." Jn 6:35 "I am the living bread that came down from heaven. If anyone eats of this bread, he will live forever. This bread is my flesh, which I will give for the life of the world." Jn 6:51 What a great invitation, but just in case we are not quite convinced, Jesus reassures us, "If I testify about myself, my testimony is not valid. There is another (God) who testifies in my favor, and I know that His testimony about me is valid." Jn 5:31-32 God confirms the claims of the Son, "This is my Son, whom I love; with Him I am well pleased. Listen to Him." Mt 17:5 Just in case we are still unconvinced, Jesus says, "If anyone chooses to do God's will, he will find out whether I speak on my own." Jn 7:17 So here we are, we have been invited to personal experience.

Based on the claims of both the Father and the Son, we should be convinced that the word of God is trustworthy, and we should take Him seriously. Nevertheless, if all that were not enough, the Psalmist, based on his experiences, invites us to try and see the rewards of a relationship with the Almighty. In Psalm 34:8, he says, "Taste and see that the Lord is good; blessed is the man who takes refuge in Him." David was a man just like us; with frailties that are common to us, but personal experience had taught him a lot about God's goodness to those who will trust Him. So David, a sinner like us is challenging us to a firsthand experience with the Living God. It is not enough to base our faith/beliefs on the experiences of others; we need to have our own experiences. The only way for one to find out if a dish is or is not good is by tasting it or eating it.

What did David know about the Lord? He knew about the Lord's faithfulness. God had him anointed to be king of Israel years before he actually became king. Between the time of his anointment and the time he actually became king, Saul pursued him relentlessly, for years, trying to kill him to secure the throne for his son, Jonathan. In all of that, David did not give up; he trusted God and His promise, and sure enough he became king. (Are you waiting for a promise to be fulfilled? Be patient, God is faithful!) During the time he was on the run, David trusted God to provide for him and his men, and God did. On numerous occasions, David sought God's guidance with specifics, and God addressed those specifics. One such occasion is recorded in 1 Sam 30:1-8. David and his men had left their wives and children back at home in Ziklag. The village was attacked, burned, and the families carried off by the raiders. David's conversation with God went like this, "Shall I pursue this raiding party? Will I overtake them?" God responded, "Pursue them, you will certainly overtake them and succeed in the rescue." 1 Sam 30:8

Also, David experienced God's forgiveness and mercy; after he had Uriah killed so he could cover up his adulterous affair with Bathsheba, Uriah's wife. God confronted him through the prophet Nathan; when he admitted his sin, God forgave him. He expressed all that in Psalm 51. Through his many encounters with God, he had firsthand knowledge that God is good. His desire is that all will come to know God as intimately as he did. Their relationship was so intimate that when David was puzzled about something, he just asked God, as friend to friend. How beautiful!

"Taste and see that the Lord is good; blessed is the man who takes refuge in Him." For those who already know the Lord, David is inviting us to know Him on a deeper level, as a friend. Jesus said, "You are my friends if you do what I command you." Jn 15:14 Having known God's goodness, we need to encourage those who have not yet experienced Him to do so. We need to do it convincingly, excitedly, lovingly! David was very sure about his experience with God; he summed it up very simply, "The Lord is good." Since we've known a measure of God's goodness, we have the same responsibility David had. We need to invite others to try out our unfailing God. Jesus said, "If anyone chooses to do God's will, he will find out whether my teaching comes from God or whether I speak on my own." Jn 7:17 We have known God's goodness on different levels, and if we can't think of anything at all to ascribe to His credit, we can definitely talk about how He chose us, and brought us out of darkness into His marvelous light. "But you are a chosen people, a royal priesthood, a holy nation, a people belonging to God, that you may **declare the praises** of Him who called you out of darkness into His wonderful light. 1 Pet 2:9

THE ARMORY

There is appropriate attire for every occasion. You most likely won't go to a wedding in a gym outfit or play basketball wearing a formal gown. Neither will the military go to war wearing a pair of shorts and a tank top.

The Christian is involved in an ongoing battle; the devil of course is the enemy. "For our struggle is not against flesh and blood, but against the rulers, against the authorities, against the powers of this dark world and against the spiritual forces of evil in the heavenly places." Eph 6:12

The Christian therefore needs to dress appropriately for the battle; he or she needs armor. "Therefore put on the full armor of God, so that when the day of evil comes, you may be able to stand your ground, and after you have done everything, to stand." Eph 6:13

The word of God has identified the armor pieces that will ensure our **safety and victory** on the battlefield. We cannot be partially clad; we have to put on the **FULL** (complete, total, whole) armor. We cannot wear it off and on, we have to be in the armor **all the time**, and also be vigilant, watching the enemy's every move.

A FULL ARMOR CONSISTS OF THE FOLLOWING (Eph 6:14-18)

Each piece has a specific function, and is therefore essential.

Belt of **truth**

Breastplate of **righteousness**

Feet fitted with the readiness that comes from the **gospel of peace**

The shield of **faith** to extinguish the flaming arrows of the evil one

The helmet of **salvation**

The sword of the spirit which is **the word of God** (learn to say to the devil, "it is written.")

Prayerfulness
Alertness

Remember, our armor was designed for us by God to ensure our on-going safety and victory in our battle against sin and the devil. It is sad to say that we don't always keep it on in readiness, and when we get caught off guard, we turn quickly to the arm of flesh. Needless to say the arm of flesh always fails, miserably. Let's rid ourselves of the arm of flesh by keeping on God's armor instead.

LIKE FATHER, LIKE CHILD

Paternity testing is a big deal for men who want to challenge the claims of mothers who have named them as their children's fathers. There are numerous reasons why these men have doubts. The test establishes or rules out paternity. In other words, there is something (genes) that links a parent and his child unquestionably. After paternity is established scientifically, there are other things that reinforce paternity. The child grows up exhibiting some of the father's traits, like features, mannerism, risk for some health issues, etc.

In the same way, there is something that proves our oneness with God, the indwelling of the Holy Spirit. When we come to faith through the finished work of Christ, He gives us the Spirit to bear witness with our spirit that we are children of God. (Rom 8:16) Anyone who does not have this witness in himself is not the child of God, and therefore can only have the devil for a father. "And if anyone does not have the Spirit of Christ, he does not belong to Christ." Rom 8:9b

A third option is unavailable; it is either Christ or the devil.

Children of God will have his nature, and that is what tells the world we are born of God. He said:

+ "I am the Lord your God; consecrate yourselves and be holy, because I am holy." Lev 11:44a

+ "God is light: in Him there is no darkness at all. If we claim to have fellowship with Him yet walk in darkness, we lie and do not live by the truth." 1 Jn 1:5b-6

+ "But the fruit of the Spirit is love, joy, peace, patience, kindness and self-control. Against such things there is no law." Gal 5:22-23

+ "No one who is born of God will continue to sin, because God's seed remains in him; he cannot go on sinning, because he has been born of God." 1 Jn 3:9

+ Then the King will say to those on His right, 'Come, you who are blessed by my Father; take your inheritance, the kingdom prepared for you since the creation of the world." Mt 25:34

Jesus warned against false prophets, giving the clue to recognizing them. He said, "They come to you in sheep's clothing, but inwardly they are ferocious wolves. **By their fruits you'll know them."** Mt 7:15b-16a

Exhibited behavior speaks volumes about a person; whereas claims about one's self say very little about him or her. A wolf will always act like a wolf regardless of its clothing because it does not know any different.

Children of the devil likewise, are also known by their deeds; the sad part is they don't tell themselves they are going to live like the devil, they just do; they have his DNA. What they do is their norm; they don't realize they are influenced by another, Satan their father.

+ Are they liars? So is their father, "You belong to your father, the devil . . . He was a murderer from the beginning, not holding to the truth, for there is no truth in him. **When he lies, he speaks his native language**, for he is a liar and the father of lies." Jn 8:44

+ Do they live in sin? So does their father, "He who does what is sinful is of the devil, because the devil has been sinning from the beginning." 1 Jn 3:8a

+ Do they pretend to be what they are not? No surprise there, "And no wonder, for Satan himself masquerades as an angel of light. It is not surprising, then, if his servants masquerade as servants of righteousness." 2 Cor 11:14-15a

+ And what is their end? "Then He will say to those on His left, 'Depart from me, you who are cursed, into the eternal fire prepared for the devil and his angels." Mt 25:41

THE CHRISTIAN AND WORRY

(Read Mt 6:25-34)

I hope you will learn this lesson with me. It is vital to a Christian's well being.

What is worry? Dictionary def—1). Make or feel anxious, 2). Seize with teeth and shake,

WHY DO WE WORRY (Non—Christian have a very good reason to worry)
1. **Ignorance**
   a. We don't always remember who we are in Christ,(**God is our FATHER**)
   b. We don't know the word like we should. "If you hold to my teaching, you are really my disciples. Then you will know the truth, and the truth will set you free." Jn 8:31-32

2. **Faith failure** Peter trying to walk on water like Christ didn't quite make it. Christ's rebuke was, "you of little faith . . . why did you doubt?' Mt 14:31b

3. **We listen to the wrong people** 'Blessed is the man who does not walk in the counsel of the wicked." Ps 1:1a
Some just enjoy worrying, they invent a reason when they don't have one.

CONSEQUENCES OF WORRY

1. Divides the mind, clouds thinking, and results in inability to make the right decisions.
2. Fragmented emotions
3. Drains energy resulting in decreased productivity
4. Pity party (woe is me, I have a BIG problem)
5. Withdrawal from people (or they withdraw from us, because they are tired of hearing about it)
6. Questioning and blaming God
7. Stop praying, may be
8. The prescription trap (see the specialist who puts you on medication to help you cope and the rest becomes history)
9. Loose our testimony (observers say "where is her God," "Isn't she a Christian?")

SOLUTION

*   Always remind ourselves that we are **ROYALTY.** God sent His Son to die for us. "But you are a chosen people, a royal priesthood, a holy nation **a people belonging to God.**" 1 Peter 2:9

*   View the problem in the context of His word. (in other words, focus on God and not the problem) "Come to me, all you who are weary and burdened, and I will give you rest" Mt 11:28 "Fear not, for I have redeemed you; I have summoned you by name; **you are mine.** When you pass through the waters, I will be with you; and when you pass through the rivers, they will not sweep over you . . . . For I am the Lord, your God, the Holy One of Israel, your Savior." Isaiah 43:1-3

*   "But seek first His kingdom and righteousness" Mt 6:33 When we seek His kingdom, we seek His kingship in our lives which should bring us to obedience to His

word. Then He will take care of the rest as He promised. Subjects always obey their king without question, so should we be in our relationship with God.

+ Worry is not befitting a Christian

+ God won't say "don't worry" if He meant for us to worry

+ He has said, "I am with you"

+ Believe that He has the power to banish all that ails us.

WORRY

I've learned another way to define worry. Here we go. When we worry, we are trying to take over Another Person's problems, without being asked. And it is an indication that the problem we are trying to solve is beyond our ability, and has not been assigned to us. Continuing to worry implies that we are impersonating the One whose responsibility we are assuming, and we are attempting to take over His Job. The last time I checked the Wanted ADs, only vacant positions were posted; God's position was not on the list, and therefore is not vacant. Nevertheless, if it were posted, nobody in this world would qualify for it.

All posted jobs have listed requirements like: training, licensure, certification, experience, etc. Likewise, if God's position were posted, the applicants would have to show proof of qualification. So in a one page document, here are the qualifications that would have to be met. The qualified applicant would have to be able to answer 'Yes' to all the following:

Have you ever spoken anything into existence?

"And God said,' Let there be light,' and there was light." Gen 1:3

Have you ever created any living thing?

"The Lord God formed the man . . . and breathed into his nostrils . . . became a living being." Gen 2:7

Have you ever raised the dead?

'Lazarus, come out." John 11:43b

Have you ever gone for an extended period of time without slumber or sleep?

"He who watches over you will not slumber." Ps 121:3b

Can you see what is going on around the world, all at the same time, every second of the day?

"The eyes of the Lord are everywhere, keeping watch on the wicked and the good." Prov 15:3

Can you tell what someone is thinking, going to say, or do before they do?

". . . You perceive my thoughts from afar . . . before a word is on my tongue you know it completely, O Lord." Ps 139:2b, 4

Did you die, and then come back to life without seeing decay?

"My body also will rest secure, . . . because you will not . . . nor will you let your Holy One see decay." Ps16:9b-10

Do you love Unconditionally, 100 percent of the time?

". . . While we were still sinners, Christ died for us." Rom 5:7-8

Do you forgive, and also forget, 100 percent of the time?

"I will forgive their wickedness and will remember their sins no more." Jer 31:34b

Can you and will you take on the punishment others deserve?

"Very rarely . . . But God demonstrates His love . . . while we were still sinners, Christ died for us." Rom 5:7-8

You are disqualified from applying, or taking over God's job if you answered 'No' to any of the above questions. The next time you have something to worry about, ask yourself, "Am I God?" If you are not God, then it's time to pray and turn over the problem to the Him who can solve it with ease. "Come to me, all you who are weary and burdened, and I will give you rest." Mt 11:28

WONDERFULLY MADE

Who are you? Where do you come from? I am a child of God, created in His image, bought by the blood of Christ. I am very special and so are you! There is none other like me or you on earth. There is no one else who looks like me, sounds like me or thinks like me.

Yes, there could be someone who looks like me, someone who sounds like me and probably someone who thinks like me. But I doubt that you will find one person who is like me in all those areas.

The psalmist says, "I praise you because I am fearfully and wonderfully made."

Ps 139:14a

Let's consider, just for a brief moment, how our bodies function. Don't you find it scary? How does your body know when to let tears flow when you hurt? How does your body know to pull away when you touch something hot? How do your mouth and teeth know solid food should be chewed and not swallowed whole, and why don't they try to chew on water? An intelligent creator designed you that way. It's simply amazing how all the body parts know their function and know how and when to interact with each other!

The other parts know it when one part is in trouble; and usually, they do whatever it takes to compensate.

Only an intelligent designer can create something as sophisticated as the human body. Consider the brain. The intelligence, the ingenuity and creativity it displays are unbelievable. The great ships on the ocean defy gravity and stay afloat. The planes in the air defy gravity and stay suspended. The cars on the road, speeding at 65 mph can come to a stop when the brakes are applied. Let's not forget the computer and all its capabilities. The human brain designed all that? Aren't we therefore fearfully and wonderfully made?

Like the Psalmist, we need to be awed by who we are, and be thankful for our uniqueness. With our uniqueness comes responsibility. First, we need to be content with whom and what we are. Do you sometimes wish you were a little taller, slightly shorter, with blue and not green eyes, etc.? God has made us the way we each are for a reason. He does not owe us any explanation or apology. I think we can safely say He made us the way we are for his pleasure and purpose. After all, "Does the clay say to the potter, 'What are you making?'" Isa 45:9b Or, "Shall what is formed say to him who formed it, 'Why did you make me like this?'" Rom 9:20b

Secondly, we need to be grateful and enjoy the fact that we are so different from each other. God in His infinite wisdom decided that's just how He wants us. We need to feel free in feeling very, very special to God (Not in an arrogant way). We also need to respect the fact that everybody else is just as special though they are different from us. So now, we are all very special people, twice as special because we've been cleansed by the blood of His Son Jesus!

WHY SHOULD WE PRAY FOR EACH OTHER?

A. WE ARE COMMANDED TO

"Therefore, confess your sins to each other and pray for each other so that you may be healed." Ja 5:16a

B. HE LEFT US AN EXAMPLE

"I pray for them, I am not praying for the world, but for those you have given me for they are yours." Jn 17:9

"M y prayer is not for them (Disciples) alone. I pray also for those who will believe in me through their message, (us) that all of them may be one." Jn 17:20-21a

". . . . I have prayed for you Simon that your faith may not fail . . ." Lk 22:32

C. SOME OF WHAT WE SHOULD PRAY FOR

DELIVERANCE

1. "And pray that we may be delivered from wicked and evil men, . . ." 2 Thes 3:2
2. Acts 12:5-16

STRENGTH IN THE MIDST OF OUR TRIALS

1. "Simon, Simon, Satan has asked to sift you as wheat, but I have prayed for you Simon, that your faith may not fail, and when you have turned back, strengthen your brothers." Lk 22:31-32

2. "So Peter was kept in prison, but the church was earnestly praying to God for him." Acts 12:5

FOR HEALING

1. "Now Simon's mother-in-law was suffering from a high fever, and they asked Jesus to help her. So he bent over her and rebuked the fever, and it left her." Lk 4:38b-39a
2. "Therefore confess your sins to each other and pray for each so that you may be healed. The prayer of a righteous man is powerful and effective." James 5:16
3. "So Moses cried out to the Lord, 'O God please heal her'." Num 12:13

FOR FORGIVENESS FOR SINS AND FAILINGS

1. "But now, please forgive their sins but if not, then blot me out of the book you have written." Ex 32:32
2. "In accordance with your great love, forgive the sin of this people . . . The Lord replied 'I have forgiven them, as you asked.'" Num 14:19-20
3. I lay prostrate . . . I prayed . . . O Sovereign Lord, do not destroy your people." Deut 9:25-26

FOR SPIRITUAL GROWTH

1. "For this reason, ever since I heard about you faith in the Lord Jesus and love for all the saints, I have not stopped giving thanks for you, remembering you in my prayers." Eph 1:15-16
2. And this is my prayer that your love may abound more and more in knowledge and depth of insight." Php 1:9

OPPORTUNITY AND EFFECTIVENESS IN WITNESS

1. "Pray for us that the message of the Lord may spread rapidly and be honored," 2 Thes 3:1

2. "And pray for us, too, that God may open a door for our message, so that we may proclaim the mystery of Christ . . . Pray that I may proclaim it clearly, as I should." Col 4:3-4

WHEN WE GET HOME

We sinners needed so desperately to be saved, so Jesus Christ came.

Our salvation cost Him pain, suffering, and humiliation; it cost Him His very life.

He endured terrible agony, but it was not for naught, it was to build a relationship with us.

He is sustaining us through His prayers and intercession, through His protection, provision, guidance, instructions, directions, chastening, encouragement, and blessings.

Then will come the crowning moment, the moment He presents us to God His Father, "faultless". It will be with "EXCEEDINGLY GREAT JOY". There will be dancing, singing, and feasting!!!

The smile on His face will say it all, "VICTORY, VICTORY, VICTORY! Victory is perfectly complete"!

Then the angels will cheer, shout, and declare, "HE did it, HE did it, HE did it. He brought them all home, Halleluiah!!"

Then with the Father seated on His throne, the Son will say to Him, "Father, these were yours and you put them trustingly in my care. Our enemy tried tirelessly to destroy them at every opportunity he found, but being the great Shepherd that I AM, I watched over them, instructed them, rebuked them, and sometimes, chastened them. I kept them from falling. Now here they are, all dressed in white; they overcame.

So Father, not having lost any of them, I present them all to you!!! They are ready, ready to each receive a crown and a mansion; ready to worship You day and night, forever, with no one to stop them or ever make them afraid.

Then the Father will say, "Welcome home my beloved, inherit the mansions that I have prepared for you. Your days of suffering and weeping are over. You will never again shed another drop of tear, you will never be sick again, and death will never again show up at your door. You will worship me forever and ever!!!

Based on Jude V 24

WAITING EXPECTANTLY

This world is not my home
It does not look anything like my home
Had it been my home, sin, suffering, and destruction will be unheard of
This world is not my home; it is full of evil and pain
It does not feel like my home, it cannot be my home

My home is far beyond the sky
It has pearly gates and streets of gold
Nothing evil will enter in
Only the redeemed may enter
Entering through the blood of Christ

My home will have no police officers or jails
Because there will be no law breakers or criminals
My home will have no hospitals or emergency rooms
My home will have only one Physician, Jesus Christ
My home is a very special place

There will be no politics, campaigns, or presidential elections
There will never be term limits or impeachments
There is one King, King of the universe
He will rule throughout eternity
My home is a wonderful place

This world is not my home
I don't feel at home here
I can't afford to be comfortable here
I want to be watching in anticipation when my Lord returns

The pain and anguish of this world help me stay focused on my home

Thank you Lord for my troubles and heartaches
They serve to remind me that I am not yet home
They make my heart yearn for your return
One day, and soon, your trumpet will sound
To gather your children home, where we will finally feel at home.
Even so, Lord Jesus, come!

MARY, DID YOU KNOW?

One of the newer Christmas songs asks this question, "Mary, did you know? Did you know that your baby boy will someday . . . ?"

I am sure her response would have been an emphatic "No." She didn't know her Son was going to walk on water, going to be treated cruelly by sinners and killed. All she knew was, God had called her to a task, and she was willing to be used. Even though she did not know the details of her calling she was willing to trust Him who called her. Her response was, "I am the Lord's servant. May it be to me as you have said." Lk 1:38

It is easy for us to want to know what lies ahead when we are called, but God does not give all the details when He calls. When He called Abraham, all He said to him was, "Leave your country, your people and your father's household and go to the land I will show you . . . and all peoples on earth will be blessed through you." Gen 12:1-3 Although the instruction sounded straight forward, Abraham experienced a lot more than he anticipated.

When He called Moses at the burning bush He didn't reveal the details of his assignment. All Moses knew was, he was charged to bring the Israelites out of Egypt. "I am sending you to Pharaoh to bring my people the Israelites out of Egypt." Ex 3:10

That assignment turned out to be more involved than he or anyone else could have imagined. He had to deal with Pharaoh's refusal, the Israelites rebellion, disobedience, idolatry and the consequences of his own display of anger. (Not permitted to go into the Promised Land)

Saul/Paul knew from the beginning of his calling that he had been called to do something, but what? All he was told was, "Now get up and go into the city, and you will be told what you must do." Acts 9:6 He had no idea what was ahead, but the accounts tell us how severely he suffered. If God reveals to us step by step what we are going to face, how likely would it be that we will go along with His plan? Out of fear, we will most likely say, "Thanks, but No thanks." If the Israelites had known what the dessert experience was going to be like, they most likely would have rather stayed in slavery.

We see from the Scriptures that all those He called He also enabled; He never left them to fend for themselves. He provided all they needed. When Abraham almost lost his wife to the Pharaoh of Egypt, God made a way for him to get her back untouched. Gen 12:10-20 When Moses needed assistance, God raised Aaron and when Saul/Paul needed a partner, He provided Silas.

Although we never know the end at the start, we need to have Mary's attitude, "I am the Lord's servant. May it be to me as you have said." Mary must have believed that God was going to work it out no matter what, and sure enough when her Son hung on the cross and her heart was broken, God provided comfort through John who took her home. "When Jesus saw His mother there, and the disciple whom He loved standing nearby, He said to His mother, 'Dear woman, here is your son,' and to the disciple, 'Here is your mother.' From that time on, this disciple took her into his house." Jn 19:26-27

Maybe the sequel to that song, "Mary did you know?" should be, "Mary, would you have?" Is God calling you to a task? Trust Him and allow Him to have His way with you!

"WHAT IS YOUR LIFE?"

Recently, I lost a very dear brother. He went from appearing and feeling okay to "I am weak" and dead in less than an hour. So "what is your life?" Ja 4:14

The answer: "You are a mist that appears for a little while and then vanishes." James 4:14b

Life is so, so short! It's been proven over and over again, but for some reason, we live as if it will never end. So knowing that life is really short, how should we live?

We should live as people who are just passing through this world; as people who have no attachments to anything here, because we'll take nothing with us when we exit. Solomon says, "Naked a man comes from his mother's womb, and as he comes, so he departs. He takes nothing from his labor that he can carry in his hand." Eccl 5:15

Job understood it when he said, "Naked I came from my mother's womb, and naked I will depart." Job 1:21a

If we are not going to live here for long, and if we are not going to take anything with us when we leave, then we need to focus on things that have eternal value. "What good will it be for a man if he gains the whole world, yet forfeits his soul?" Mt 16:26

Material things enhance our living, but we need to avoid hoarding them. We need to be willing to part with them if we have to. Let's not spend all our energies chasing things, competing with others and envying those who have more than we do. The word we should keep in mind in all circumstances is, 'contentment'. God will always provide; He will never leave us alone. He promised! Paul's secret for contentment was that, he knew he could do all things through Christ who strengthened him. (Php 4:11a-13)

Talking about contentment, Paul again wrote, "But godliness with contentment is great gain. For we brought nothing into the world, and we can take nothing out of it. But if we have food and clothing, we will be content with that . . . . For the love of money is a root of all kinds of evil." 1 Tim 6:6-10a

Some of the evil referred to could be, lying, cheating, stealing and even murder. Had King David been content with all the wives and concubines he had, he would not have committed adultery and murder. May God help us to be a contented and thankful people.

Let's consider the effects of anxiety on our lives. It can paralyze us and make us physically and emotionally sick. Anxiety robs us of joy, peace, the ability to see things from God's perspective and the ability to be thankful. The irony of anxiety is that we might not live long enough to go through what we are anxious about. But if we live long enough to go through it, God will walk us through it. "When you pass through the waters, I will be with you; and when you pass through the rivers, they will not sweep over you." Isa 43:2a

Our life's like vapor, when it evaporates, only one thing remains, and that is our relationship with the Lord. Let's cultivate it.

WHAT IS HINDERING YOUR CHRISTIAN WALK?

Therefore, since we are surrounded by such a great cloud of witnesses, let us throw off **everything that hinders** and **the sin that so easily entangles**, and let us run with perseverance the race marked out for us. Let us fix our eyes on Jesus, the author and perfecter of our faith." Heb 12:1-2a

Let us do a little soul searching.

I am sure we will agree with Paul when he says, "For what I do is not the good I want to do: no, the evil I do not want to do—this I keep on doing." Rom 7:19

There is something that is keeping our light dim (Weight and sin). It might not be the same issue for everybody, but whatever it is, we need to lay it aside. People who run marathons do not carry anything, the less weight they carry, the faster they run.

1. LET US EACH IDETENTIFY WHAT IS HINDERING OUR TESTIMONY

Are any of these your downfall?

GOSSIP (our work environment makes this a big issue, let us be vigilant, pray for one another and hold each other accountable. We need to break that habit)
PRIDE (How do you respond when you are offended?)
ARROGANCE
UNFORGIVING SPIRIT
UNHELPFULNESS
CHEATING
LYING
ETC, ETC

2. AGREE IT IS DESTROYING YOUR TESTIMONY, ASK FOR HELP

"Woe to me! . . . I am ruined! For I am a man of unclean lips, and I live among a people of unclean lips . . ." Isaiah 6:5

"What a wretched man I am! Who will rescue me from this body of death?" Rom 7:24

3. SHARE YOUR CONCERNS WITH ANOTHER

"Therefore, confess your sins to each other so that you may be healed. The prayer of a righteous man is powerful and effective." Ja 5:16

4. PURPOSE IN YOUR HEART TO WORK ON THAT ISSUE

"But Daniel resolved not to defile himself with the royal food and wine." Dan 1:8 (and he didn't)

5. FOLLOW THROUGH

"I can do everything through Him who gives me strength." Php 4:13

"Without wood a fire goes out: without gossip a quarrel dies down." Prov 26:20 (memorize)

"WHAT ARE YOU DOING?"

"What are you doing?" This sounds like a very reasonable question to ask another person when you don't understand what they are doing or why. However the tone of your voice and your body language can convey your deepest feelings about what they are doing.

Depending on how you pose this question, you could be suggesting, they are doing it wrong, they are incompetent, you are in disagreement and you know a better way of doing it.

You may or may not get a response to your question, depending on how the other person perceives the situation. You might get an answer to your enquiry because you sounded genuinely interested. On the other hand, you might not because you came across as nosy, judgmental, a 'know it all' and even condemning.

As Christians, when we go through trials and difficulties, we quickly find ourselves in a "What are you doing, God?" mode. Most often, we get no immediate answers. As long as our response to our circumstances is not an expression of gratitude to God for being in control of our lives, we are expressing disagreement. We are in essence saying to Him, "God, are you sure this is what you want to do?" "Is this the right thing to do?" "Shouldn't you do it this other way?" "Do you know the outcome of this?" "Let me tell you, you are making a big mistake." How ridiculous! How disrespectful!

"Does the clay say to the potter, 'What are you making?' Does your work say, 'He has no hands'? Woe to him who says to his father, 'What have you begotten?' or to his mother, 'What have you brought to birth?'" Isa 45:9b-10

"Shall what is formed say to Him who formed it, 'He did not make me'? Can the pot say of the potter, 'He knows nothing'"? Isa 29:16b (Which is what we imply when we disagree with God).

There has never been a dialogue between a potter and the clay. The potter can fashion it into anything he chooses, vessel of honor or of dishonor. The potter owes the clay no explanation. The clay is his, and he fashions it in a way that brings him pleasure and serves the purpose that he desires.

God is the potter and we are the clay. He is free to do with us as He pleases. He owes us no explanation or apologies. However, we can be sure of one thing; His plans for us are for our welfare, not to harm us. Jer 29:11

We question God because we desire a pain-free life. He never promised us an easy Christian life; rather, right from the beginning He told us, "If anyone would come after me, he must deny himself and take up his cross and follow me." Lk 9:23 Again, "Anyone who does not take his cross and follow me is not worthy of me." Mt 10:38

With the reminder of suffering along the way, He assures us of His strength and ability to help us overcome. "And God is faithful; He will not let you be tempted beyond what you can bear. But when you are tempted, He will also provide a way out so that you can stand up under it." 1 Cor 10:13
In addition to enabling us, He comforts us. "Praise be to the God and Father of our Lord Jesus Christ, the Father of compassion and the God of all comfort, who comforts us in all our troubles. 2 Cor 1:3-4a

"For the Lord comforts His people." Isa 49:13b

"I, even I, am He who comforts you." Isa 51:12a

"As a mother comforts her child, so I will comfort you." Isa 66:13a

MEMORIZE—"Like clay in the hand of the potter, so are you in my hand." Jer 18:6b

WE ARE SURE

"I write these things to you who believe in the name of the Son of God (Jesus) so that you may **know** that you have eternal life." 1 Jn 5:13

This verse is so refreshing! Despite the chaos we see and read about, we are not afraid or discouraged; instead we have hope. This is hope that no one can take away from us, because it is based on God's word which is true. In the event that we lose everything and even our lives, one thing is certain—eternal life!

Jesus is gone to prepare a place for us, and then He will come back and take us to Himself so that we also will be where He is. Jn 14:2b-3

There are people who are **wishing and hoping** that someday, based on their good deeds, God will say to them, "You did okay; you made it, come into heaven." But when is good, good enough and how much of good is good enough? What a risky way to approach eternity, leaving it to chance! Why wait till the end to find out? What will people do when at the end He says to them, "Sorry, your efforts were not good enough"?

Nevertheless, those who are trusting in anything other than Christ will hear Him say something along that line, because His word clearly says, "For it is by grace you have been saved, through faith—and this not from yourselves, it is the gift of God—not by works, so that no one can boast." Eph 2:8-9

No boasting in heaven!! Our good deeds, we are told; are like filthy rags. They cannot enter heaven.

We don't know what the next minute, hour, day, week or year holds but we know Him who is in control of all things. Let's not worry or panic about troubles. In fact He says to us, "When these things begin to take place, stand up and lift up your heads, because your redemption is drawing near." Lk 21:28

It is nearer now than when we first believed. Rom 13:11b

As we rejoice in the assurance of eternal life, let us show concern for those who are not so sure about their future. We need to be afraid for them because as our redemption draws close, so does their doom.

Unless we pray and witness diligently, many loved ones will go to a Christ-less eternity. We need to do it while we still have breath, health and time. Soon it will be too late; the opportunity would have been forever lost.

MEMORIZE: "As long as it is day, we must do the work of Him who sent me. Night is coming, when no one can work." Jn 9:4

UNPROFITABLE ARGUMENTS

Do you ever get caught in arguments regarding your faith?

The Bible teaches that such arguments do not profit.

There is a difference between someone who is genuinely interested in knowing the truth and someone who wants an argument for the sake of arguing.

Take time with someone who really wants to know, and be patient with them. Explain what you know, and if unsure of yourself, just say so rather than misleading them. Take time to research the information and follow up with them later, and don't forget to pray for them.

If you sense that someone is trying to engage you in a discussion just to prove how much they know or to blaspheme your God, your best defense is to refuse to be engaged, ask to be excused, and don't forget to pray for them.

The following verses should help us:

". . . command certain men not to teach false doctrines any longer **nor to devote themselves to myths and endless genealogies. These promote controversies rather than God's work—which is by faith."** 1 Tim 1:3b-4

"Have nothing to do **with godless myths and old wives' tales;** rather, train yourself to be Godly." 1 Tim 4:7

"If anyone teaches false doctrines and does not agree to the sound instruction of our Lord Jesus Christ and to godly teaching, he is conceited and understands nothing. He has an **unhealthy interest in controversies and quarrels about words that result in envy, strife, malicious talk, evil suspicions and constant friction between men of corrupt mind . . ."** 1 Tim 6:3-4

"Don't have anything to do with **foolish and stupid arguments, because you know they produce quarrels.** And the Lord's servant must not quarrel; instead, he must be kind to everyone, able to teach, not resentful. Those who oppose him, he must **gently instruct,** in the hope that God will grant them repentance leading them to a knowledge of the truth, and that they will come to their senses and escape from the trap of the devil, who has taken them captive to do his will." 2 Tim 2:23-26

"**But avoid foolish controversies and genealogies and arguments and quarrels about the law, because these are unprofitable and useless.**" Titus 3:9

UNFADING BEAUTY

Beauty is defined as the quality present in a thing or person that gives intense pleasure or deep satisfaction to the mind, whether arising from sensory manifestations (as shape, color, sound, etc.), a meaningful design or pattern, or something else (as a personality in which high spiritual qualities are manifest).

Beauty is a sought after quality among the young as well as the old, among both male and female. There is nothing wrong with beauty, and it is okay to seek to be beautiful, but the kind of beauty one puts emphasis on or pursues is a measure of one's value system.

There are two kinds of beauty, outward beauty and inward beauty. Each kind is visible to observers. Both need maintenance, but only one has the potential to last a lifetime. One fades with time regardless of diligent maintenance while the other gets better with time and diligent maintenance.

The outward beauty is the look that is based on physical appearance, how it is dressed up, and how it is presented to self and to others. The average person likes to look beautiful and presentable, and we all should. Outward beauty is financially costly, because of the cost of the things that go into creating beauty. Included are things like, food and nourishment, clothes, health, physical fitness, makeup and sometimes surgery, which all come with a price tag. The price is higher for some than it is for others. Physical beauty in itself can be short-lived because of accidents, diseases and other health issues. For some, as aging sets in, maintenance cost goes up significantly. Cosmetic surgery is now a booming business in an effort to keep people young and beautiful, for longer.

Inward beauty on the other hand has a spiritual origin, and does get better with time. Inward beauty starts with being born again, when an individual understands and admits he or she is a sinner, asks Jesus for the forgiveness of sins, and asks Him to be Lord and Master of their life. Jesus responds by forgiving, and coming to indwell the individual in the person of the Holy Spirit. He or she becomes a new creature, and through reading and studying the word of God, his or her mind is renewed, and begins to radiate the beauty and fragrance of Christ. This transformation is a life-long spiritual process. The longer we read and study and apply the truths to living, our inward beauty becomes evident, becoming better with the passage of time. Financial cost is at a minimum; the cost of a Bible, time to read, study, pray and fellowship. Both kinds of beauty are necessary, but let's remember that inward beauty far outweighs outward beauty in God's calculations. If we have the mind of Christ, we will evaluate beauty His way.

"Your beauty should not come from outward adornment, such as braided hair and the wearing of gold jewelry and fine clothes. Instead, it should be that of your inner self, the unfading beauty of a gentle and quiet spirit, which is of great worth in God's sight." 1 Pet 3:3-4

TRUST AND OBEY

Recently, I needed direction to get home from a doctor's office (first visit of course). The receptionist said to me, "Go out, make a right turn, and another right at the traffic light and that should be it." So I did. When I got to that last right turn, I expected it to say, 50 West, but it didn't; instead it said something like 556. I hesitated to make that turn, but decided to make it any way and see what would happen. A mile or so down that road, the signs started to say, you guessed it, 50 West.

Although the Road Sign was confusing, the receptionist really knew what she was talking about. Had I not followed her directions, I would have been very lost. She did not explain that Route 556 was going to turn into Route 50 West further down that road.

Then it dawned on me, God doesn't always give us details or explanations, but we just need to follow His directions in order to get to the desired destination. We can choose to trust the Lord with all our hearts or lean on our own understanding. (Prov 5:5-6) Which ever choice we make will have a different result. When I followed the direction even when it didn't make sense, I got home with no problems. If I had gone in another direction, I would have ended up farther away from home, wasted gas and have been very frustrated.

The Lord admonished the Israelites to choose life/blessing by following Him or death/curse by going their own way. "See, I am setting before you today a blessing and a curse—the blessing if you obey the commands of the Lord your God that I am giving you today; the curse if you disobey the commands of the Lord your God and turn from the way that I command you . . ." Deut 11:26-28

I don't think any of us desires the curse or death, but for some reason we deceive ourselves into thinking we know what we are doing, where we are going and how to get there. Needless to say we so often end up in trouble because of the choices we make. We enjoy calling the shots, we want to be in control of our own destiny even though we have no idea what the bigger picture looks like. It is safe to follow the Lord's leading because He knows the end from the beginning and all that is between. Trusting and obeying is not a guarantee for a trouble-free life. What it means is that we are in the center of His will and that He is in control and will provide the wisdom, strength and discernment to get through. Not a single sparrow falls to the ground without His knowledge

The Hymnist also wrote, "Trust and obey, for there's no other way to be happy in Jesus, but to trust and obey." We can't obey Him if we don't trust Him.

TIME IS LIMITED

How many people really feel the need to accomplish all they can, as quickly as they can, while they can? Are there statistics that address this type of issue? I don't know, but I am almost sure if there were, those individuals will be in the minority.

For Christians, the sense of urgency needs to be at the forefront of our thinking and planning. God has put us here on earth, at different places and in different environments to accomplish certain tasks; however, our assigned tasks did not come with specified allotted time. Since we don't know how much time we have, we need to work at a fast pace. There are variables that could interrupt or halt our work, consequently affecting our effectiveness and productivity. These variables could be in the form of declining health and abilities, changing circumstances, opened doors that close, death, and most importantly, the Lord's return.

In early spring, a little warmth brings out the tulips, and yes they are beautiful, but disappointingly, they fade away rather quickly. The azaleas bloom beautifully also, but last just as briefly. Even though they are here for such short time, they do bloom beautifully for the time they are here. Likewise we need to work at our calling enthusiastically, diligently, and prayerfully remembering that we have limited time in which to accomplish our calling. Once our time is up, it's up; we cannot undo, redo, or get extension on time.

In Proverbs 27:1, we are admonished not to "boast about tomorrow," the reason being, "you do not know what a day may bring forth." So since we have no idea what a particular day is going to be like, we need to consider each day, potentially as our last, and therefore aim at accomplishing all we possibly can. If by God's grace we see the following day, our attitude, enthusiasm, and excitement should be a repeat of the previous day, but if we never see another day, we would have done our best, not regretting missed opportunities and opened doors.

James tells us "Now listen, you who say, 'Today or tomorrow we will go to this or that city, spend a year there, carry on business and make money.' Why, you do not even know what will happen tomorrow. What is your life? You are a mist that appears for a little while and then vanishes." Ja 4:13-14 So is there anything we are putting off that we could accomplish for the Lord, today? Have you been putting off tithing until???? Are you planning to start witnessing to that neighbor next spring?? Are you going to invite that couple to Church today or next week? Tomorrow isn't really ours. We may or may not be well and alive by then, and if we were, they may not. The Preacher sums it up this way, "Since no man knows the future, who can tell him what is to come? No man has the power over the wind to contain it, so no one has power over the day of his death." Ecc 8:7-8

Matthew 24 tells us in v 36 and v 42: "No one knows about the day or hour, not even the angels in heaven, nor the Son, but only the Father." "Therefore keep watch, because you do not know on what day your Lord will come." The Lord may come any day now to rupture the Church, temporarily halting all Christian activity. Whatever is incomplete will remain incomplete. So like the tulips, let's bloom beautifully, while we can, and for as long as we can!

THINK ON THESE THINGS

"Finally, brothers, whatever is true, whatever is noble, whatever is right, whatever is pure, whatever is lovely, whatever is admirable— if anything is excellent or

Praiseworthy—think about such things." Php 4:8

Our minds can become workshops for the devil if we allow him. The word of God therefore instructs us to saturate our minds with things that are wholesome.

Things we saturate our minds with come from, things we see hear and read. They are also the things we pass on to others for their edification or defilement. Because the word says, "out of the overflow of the heart the mouth speaks. The good man brings good things out of the good stored up in him, and the evil man brings evil things out of the evil stored up in him." Mt 12:34b-35

1.   **SIGHT** What kind of movies (entertainments) do you watch? Do you feel edified by them? Would you unashamedly share it with someone else? Change channels if you have to. And if there is no clean entertainment, do without.

2.   **HEARING** What we hear stays with us for a long time, so what are we listening to? Good music, bad music, bad gossip, dirty jokes, etc. May be we should walk away when we sense we are about to hear something that is not; noble, lovely, true, right, pure etc.

3.   **READING** What do you read? Does it edify you? Increase needed knowledge.
     Is it something you can share to cheer someone up, encourage, bless or help?

What you should be reading more than anything else, is the word of God. It is amazing the wealth of information you find in there. It shows you the way of salvation, growth in the faith, all aspects of Christian living, God, God, and God. Anything you want to know regarding life is found in the Bible.

It is also very entertaining. You smile reading it, sometimes you laugh out loud, you bless God, and you think about others and pray for them. It is amazing! Make a habit of reading it every day; needless to say, you will be blessed.

MEMORIZE—"Finally, brothers, whatever is true, whatever is noble, whatever is right, whatever is pure, whatever is lovely, whatever is admirable—if anything is excellent or praiseworthy—think about such things." Php 4:8

THE WILL OF GOD

What do we really mean when we express the desire and pray to know God's will for our lives? Is it because we desperately want to do His will? The Bible says, "God has no pleasure in fools." Ecc. 5:4 We should either say it because we mean it or don't say it at all. It sounds very spiritual to say that, but what purpose does it serve if deep down in our hearts what we really want is our own will?

King Saul knew God's will when he went to fight the Amalekites. "Now go, attack the Amalekites and **totally destroy everything** that belongs to them. **Do not spare** them; . . ." 1 Sam 15:3 However, he allowed his greed and that of his fighting men to prevent him from carrying out the instructions he was given. "But Saul and the army spared Agag and the best of the sheep and cattle, the fat calves and lambs—everything that was good." 1 Sam 15:9a

Saul considered his half-hearted obedience as 'Job Accomplished.' He said to Samuel, ". . . I have carried out the Lord's instructions." V 13b "But I did obey the Lord, I went on the mission the Lord assigned me. I completely destroyed the Amalekites **and brought back** Agag their king." V20 Samuel of course explained to the king, "To obey is better than sacrifice, and to heed is better than the fat of rams." V22b We need to obey completely in all things because God does not grade on the curve. In Revelation, He said to the Church in Ephesus who was doing only some things right, "Repent and do . . . if you do not repent, I will come to you and remove your lampstand from its place." Rev 2:5b

Then there is the story of Balaam the prophet who knew clearly God's will concerning king Balak's request to curse the Israelites. God specifically said to him, "Do not go with them. You must not put a curse on those people, because they are blessed." Num 22:12

Balak sent a second delegation to entice Balaam, promising a handsome reward. Instead of standing his ground, Balaam toyed with the idea that God might change His mind. Num 22:19 When he was confronted by the angel he acted as if he didn't know anything was wrong. He said to the angel, "Now if you are displeased, I will go back." V34b What didn't he understand when God said, "You must not put a curse on those people, because they are blessed."?

What do we mean when we repeat the Lord's Prayer and say, "Your will be done on earth as it is in heaven."? Mt 6:10 I believe in heaven, God's will is carried out with precision, no questions asked, in a timely manner, with joy and enthusiasm. May this be our attitude towards God's will! Jesus knew the Father's will for Him was the cross, so he trustingly accepted it. "Not my will but yours be done." Lk 22:42

The next time we express interest in God's will, let's ask ourselves if we really want His will or simply want Him to adopt our will and bless it. Not doing things His way has consequences. King Saul lost the kingdom to David and Balaam almost died at the hand of the angel, had his donkey not seen and avoided the angel.

THE POWER OF GOD IN THE LIFE OF A CHRISTIAN

Let's see how the power of God can enable us to live victoriously in this life. **"I can do everything through Him who gives me strength." Php 4:13**

1. **OVERCOME SIN**

   "I write this to you so that you will not sin. But if anybody does sin, we have one who speaks to the Father in our defense—Jesus Christ, the Righteous One." 1 Jn 2:1 "No one who lives in Him keeps sinning. No one who continues to sin has either seen Him or known Him." 1 Jn 3:6

2. **RIGHTEOUS LIVING**

   "Whoever claims to live in Him must walk as Jesus did." 1 Jn 2:6 "He who does what is right is righteous, just as He is righteous. He who does what is sinful is of the devil, because the devil has been sinning from the beginning." 1 Jn 3:8

3. **LOVE**

   "Whoever does not love does not know God, because God is love."1 Jn 4:8 "Whoever loves his brother lives in the light, and there is nothing in him to make him stumble." 1 Jn 2:10

4. **FORGIVE**

   "Be kind and compassionate to one another, forgiving each other, just as in Christ God forgave you." Eph 4:32

"Bear with each other and forgive whatever grievances you may have against one another. Forgive as the Lord forgave you." Col 3:13

5. **COMPASSION** (sympathy or pity that moves us to help)
   "Jesus stopped and called them. 'What do you want me to do for you?' He asked. 'Lord,' they answered, 'we want our sight.' Jesus had compassion on them and touched their eyes." Mt 20:32-33

6. **ENDURE TRIALS/SICKNESS**
   "My grace is sufficient for you, for my power is made perfect in weakness." 2 Cor 12:9

7. **DILIGENCE**
   "Whatever you do, work at it with all your heart, as working for the Lord, not for men." Col 3:23

GOD, THE POWER BEHIND ALL THINGS

"Unless the Lord builds the house, its builders labor in vain. Unless the Lord watches over the city, the watchmen stand guard in vain." Ps 127:1

Can we exclude God from any aspect of our lives? Some think so. I actually met someone who thinks depending on God is a sign of weakness. As Christians, we sometimes unknowingly fall into the same trap, by making a distinction between relevant and irrelevant needs to bring to God in prayer. We treat some needs as trivial and therefore neglect to bring them to Him.

Is your safety on the road guaranteed based on the following?

- You passed a driving test
- Obtained a driver's license
- Have driving experience
- Have a car that runs pretty good
- On the road with careful drivers
- Obeying all the traffic laws?

Of course not! These things help tremendously, but are you sure everyone out there is licensed? How do you know who is driving tired or drunk? Do you anticipate someone's hubcap racing towards you from nowhere? Sometimes we can even be a danger to ourselves and others. When we get on the road, let's remember; only God can keep us safe. Let's pray! "Unless the Lord builds the house, its builders labor in vain."

Do you feel safe in your house because:

- You've locked your doors (you should lock your doors)
- You have a working smoke detector (you should have one)
- You have a security alarm system installed (won't hurt)

Remember, "Unless the Lord watches over the city, the watchmen stand guard in vain."

Do you base your recovery from illness on any of the following?

- It's just a virus
- There is a known cure
- My doctor is good

Again remember, God said to the Israelites, "I am the Lord, who heals you." Ex 15:26b

When you come up with a brilliant idea about something, do you think it's all you? Again, "Whether you turn to the right or to the left, your ears will hear a voice behind you, saying, "This is the way; walk in it." Isa 30:21

We can go on and on to prove that we need God in every situation; let's be prayerful about every area of our lives. He has said, "Apart from me you can do nothing."

Jn 15:5b

Let's always remember to be thankful; ascribing to Him the glory He deserves. We should not steal His glory or ascribe it to another. He says, "I am the Lord; that is my name! I will not give my glory to another or my praise to idols." Isa 42:8

"I will not yield my glory to another." Isa 48:11b

THE POTTER AND THE CLAY

Lord, you are the potter, I am the clay
Lovingly, you have fashioned me
Indeed, I am wonderfully and fearfully made
Lord, you are the potter, I am the clay
Not only have you fashioned me, you have fashioned me for a purpose
Being the potter, you have the right to do with me as you please
Yet in that right, you are kind and compassionate

Lord, you are the potter, I am the clay
You have lovingly chosen a path for me
Your infinite wisdom allows you to choose for me the best
Following that path draws me closer to you and to the fulfillment of your purpose
Lord, you are the potter, I am the clay
Help me stay on that path willingly, obediently and joyfully with no complaints or regrets

Lord, you are the potter, I am the clay
I do not always smile on the path, even though I know you chose it for me
Sometimes, I am scared; I hurt and cry, and wish things were different
Lord, you are the potter, I am the clay
Dare I question your wisdom and judgment?
O wretched man that I am who will deliver me from this arrogance
The arrogance of wanting something different than you intend for me

Lord, you are the potter, I am the clay
Can I or anybody else do better for me than you have done?
Do I have the right to say, "Why have you or have you not?" in any circumstance
Lord, you are the potter, I am the clay
You put your Son Jesus, through pain and suffering, for a purpose
Through that suffering, He became the only mediator between God and man
Lord, indeed you are the potter, I am the clay

Lord, you are the potter, I am the clay
With all your wisdom, power and authority
You do not trivialize my pain and heartache
You have always come alongside with comfort and sometimes, explanation
You've said, "My grace is sufficient for you, my strength is made perfect in weakness"
And with the comfort you comfort me; you want me to comfort others
O! Lord, my Lord, you are the potter with the perfect plan!

SAVING 'JESUS' WITH CONFIDENCE

As Christians, the name 'Jesus' is all we need to be able to face every situation with calmness and confidence. There is power in the name of the Lord, and that is why He gave us the authority to use it; a blank check we might say. So let's invoke it in faith. Invoking the name without faith does not do us any good. In Matthew 9:27-29 two blind men begged Jesus for healing. He asked them if they believed He could heal them, "Yes, Lord," they responded. Jesus then said to them, "According to your faith will it be done to you." Faith, even as small as a mustard seed will bring the power of God to bear.

Why is His name so powerful? It's because, He came into a sinful world, took on the nature of a servant, humbled Himself, became obedient to death-even death on the cross. As a result, God exalted Him to the highest place and gave Him **the name that is above every name.** (Php 2:7b-9)

About Him, God said, "Your throne O God, will last forever and ever and righteousness will be the scepter of your kingdom." Heb 1:4

We need to start with the understanding that, "Salvation is found in no one else, for there is **no other name** under heaven given to men by which we must be saved." Acts 4:12 "And everyone who calls on the name of the Lord will be saved." Joel 2:32, Rom 10:13

Jesus proved that truth by allowing us to experience the new birth, guaranteeing our passage from death to life. By calling on **His name** we are cleansed from all sins, past, present and future and our names written in the Lamb's book of life.

It seems to me that the most seemingly impossible miracle there could ever be is the miracle of the transformation of the human heart. It is unexplainable! Even Nicodemus, a Pharisee, a member of the Jewish ruling council had a hard time understanding it. Jesus explained it to him this way, "The wind blows wherever it pleases. You hear its sound, but you cannot tell where it comes from or where it is going. So it is with everyone born of the Spirit." Jn 3:8

Now then, if believing in Jesus' name can bring about such a dramatic change, (headed for hell one moment, heaven-bound the next) then definitely, nothing else, asked **in His name** according to His will, will be impossible.

The seventy two disciples Jesus sent out by twos returned with this report, "Lord, even the demons submit to us **in your name**." Lk 10:17b

Like these disciples, we can be victorious **in the name of Jesus**! We have the power; let's use it to thwart the devil's plans and bring glory to God.

MEMORIZE: "My Father will give you whatever you ask **in my name**." Jn 16:23b

209

THE MANUFACTURER'S MANUAL

I recently spent four painful hours at Sears Auto Center waiting to get my car serviced. I had been hearing a buzzing noise when the fan is on, so I took it in to have it checked out to avoid further damage. When the mechanic finally got around to taking a look at the car, he called me to show me what was causing the noise. I had accidentally turned off the vent on the driver's side of the car, preventing the air from flowing out of the vent. Thankfully, I was not charged for the servicing of my ignorance. On my way home, I thought, "It would have been helpful to know what the User Manual says." Knowing would have spared me the concern that something was wrong with the car when nothing was really wrong, and also, it would have saved me four precious hours. Who has that kind of time to waste? If I had been very familiar with the User Manual, I wouldn't have had to visit Sears Auto Center.

In the same way, God has given Christians a manual, the Bible, by which to live. Everything we ever need to know about Him, His plans and intentions for us and the world are clearly stated in it. "Your word is a lamp to my feet and a light for my path." Ps 119:105 The Bible, like a gold mine, has to be deeply and intentionally mined, in order to be able to find the riches that are placed in its pages. When Jesus talked about how He had searched high and low to find us, His lost sheep, He indicated the need to search diligently and tirelessly. (Lk 15) That is how we need to search the scriptures, diligently, with a ravenous appetite for knowledge. No Christian should base his/her knowledge of the scriptures solely on what is read and preached in church or at other Christian gatherings. We need to study it personally and in private, allowing the Holy Spirit to explain and show us how to apply what we read to our lives. "Open my eyes that I may see wonderful things in your law." Ps 119:18

The Scripture covers every area of our lives, and in order to find out, we have to read and study it. It will be far better to know what the Scriptures say about issues before situations arise requiring the knowledge of the mind of God. If I had read my car manual ahead of time, I would have probably been able to figure out the cause of the problem. When we don't know God's manual, we deprive ourselves of His peace and comfort in the midst of whatever we go through. One simple verse that should always comfort us is, "I will never leave you alone." Jos 1:5b If we never remember verses like that, we'll always be fearful and panicky. The word 'NEVER' should remind us of His presence in all situations. When we treat the Scriptures haphazardly, we open ourselves up to the devil's lies, and run the risk of being misled. With all the lies through the false prophets out there, we need to know the Scriptures well. No one can ever know too much Scripture. The more we study, the more we discover, the more we learn, and the more we grow. We need to go from one level of maturity to another.

THE LORD'S PRAYER FOR THE BELIEVER

(Please read John 17: 6-26)

I find it very encouraging to know that Christ prayed for me before I was ever born, before I became a Christian. Look closely at v 20, "My prayer is not for them alone. I pray also for those who will believe in me (you and I included) through their message."

So what was the focus of His prayer?

1. **PROTECTION** To be kept in the world but protected by the power of God's name, from the world and also from the evil one. V 11, 16

2. **COMPLETE UNITY** (v 11, 21, 23). We need to be united in purpose, to accomplish the Lord's purpose for the church through prayer and godly living. Our unity will be proof to the world that Christ was sent by God.

3. **FULL MEASURE OF CHRIST'S JOY** (v 13). Knowing what Christ has done for us, the salvation of our souls, should keep us constantly joyful.

4. **SANCTIFICATION** (to make holy) by the truth which is the word of God. Let us read the word of God and allow it to transform us into His image.

5. **BE MESSENGERS** (v 20). It is Christ's desire that no one should perish. He has therefore given us the task

of witnessing to others. We have to carry on the work of the Disciples, for whom He prayed. If they had not obeyed the command to go, we might never have heard the gospel. There is room for many, many more. Let's pray for many and look for opportunities to help them understand His love and sacrifice for the world.

6. **BE WITH CHRIST AND SEE HIS GLORY** (v 24) what a beautiful plea, "Father, I want those you have given me to be with me where I am and to see my glory . . ." Guess what, someday we will be with Him, "even so Lord Jesus come."

7. **GOD'S LOVE TO ABIDE IN US** (v 26) His love abiding in us enables us to love one another and all those we encounter.

MEMORIZE "Therefore He is able to save completely those who come to God through Him, because He always lives to intercede for them." Heb 7:25

THE LIVE DICTIONARY (The Bible)
DEFINITION OF LOVE

Dictionary: A book that lists the words of a language in alphabetical order and gives their meaning, or that gives the equivalent words in a . . .

The Bible is also a book, but one of the differences between the dictionary and the Bible is that, the Bible defines the word through demonstration.

The Bible Defines Love:
Love assesses the needs of others and finds ways to meet them. God knew we are sinners, He knew His nature demanded justice, but He also knew there was no way we could pay the penalty for our sins, so He sent his ONLY SON to remedy the situation.
"For God so loved the world, He gave His only begotten Son that whosoever believes in Him should not perish but have everlasting life" Jn 3:16
Jesus loved us so He gave his life, willingly, for us. In reference to laying down His life, He said, "No one takes it from me, but I lay it down of my own accord." Jn 10:18
As Jesus commanded His disciples to love one another, He explained that it was the kind of love He had for them (us), "My command is this: Love each other **as I have loved you."** Jn 15:12 He further explained, "Greater love has no one than this, that He lay down his life for his friends." Jn 15:13

214

Love makes no distinction between foe and friend. Jesus told a story about a traveler who was attacked by thieves; they stripped him of everything, beat him, and left him half dead. A priest, a Levite, and a Samaritan passed that way. Of all the people who went by that way, only the Samaritan, the supposed enemy, stopped to help the wounded. Lk 10:30-35 "While we were still sinners (God's enemies), Christ died for us" Rom 5:8b

John tells us, "This is how we know what love is: Jesus Christ laid down His life for us. And we ought to lay down our lives for our brothers." 1 Jn 3:16 For life application, John goes on to say, "If anyone has material possessions and sees his brother in need but has no pity on him, how can the love of God be in him? Dear children, let us not love with words or tongue but with actions and in truth." 1 Jn 3:17-18

The disciples had been fishing all night, and were very exhausted, but had caught nothing. Jesus knowing how tired they were, waited for them on the beach with a hot breakfast. Yes He assessed their need and met it.

In chapter 13 (V 1b-5) of the gospel of John we read, "Having loved His own who were in the world, He now showed them the **full extent** of His love." This He did by washing His disciples' feet. God the Master washed the dirty feet of the disciples. It should have been the other way around. Jesus didn't just talk about love, He demonstrated the full extent of His love by doing for others what we sinners might hesitate to do.

God has explained and demonstrated love in practical ways and bids us to, "Go and do likewise." Lk 10:37b

THE LIVE DICTIONARY DEFINITION OF SERVE

SERVE: (Dictionary def.) Perform duties or services for (another person or organization); to be a servant to, or to prepare and offer (eg. Food).

Who should serve? Traditionally, servants serve their masters and mistresses. They cook, clean, shop, garden, etc. One does not need to be a paid servant to serve. Jesus washed the disciples' feet, and then explained to them, "You call me 'Teacher' and 'Lord,' and rightly so, for that is what I am. Now that I, your Lord and Teacher, have washed your feet, you also should wash one another's feet. I have set you an example that you should do as I have done for you." Jn 13:13-15 In John 21, we are told how Jesus cooked breakfast on the beach for the disciples after they had worked all night and caught nothing. When they returned to shore, Jesus their Lord, Teacher, and Master, had breakfast ready for them. "Jesus said to them, come and have breakfast." V 12a How willing are you to serve others? Do you consider the task of serving others to be beneath you? Would you rather be served by others? Do you feel too important to serve others? So who should serve? I need to serve and you do too, because Jesus said so.

Whom should we serve? We need to serve each other; "You also should wash **one another's** feet." **and anyone** who needs to be served, "Whatever you did for one of the least of these brothers of mine you did for me." Mt 25:40b

What should our attitude be toward Serving? If Jesus were here physically, with what attitude will we serve Him? I am sure we will be excited at the opportunity; we will serve joyfully, wholeheartedly, and be grateful for the opportunity. "Serve wholeheartedly, as **if you were serving the Lord, not men.**" Eph 6:7 "Anyone who does not love his brother, whom he has seen, cannot love God whom he has not seen . . . Whoever loves God must also love his brother" I Jn 4: 20b-21 We should expect nothing in return for serving, even if we have been promised something: "So you also, when you have done everything you were told to do, should say, 'We are unworthy servants; we have only done **our duty.**'" Lk 17:10

Rewards of Service: We will be with Jesus, and God will honor us. "Whoever serves me must follow me; and where I am, my servant also will be. My Father will honor the one who serves me." Jn 12:26 "Come, you who are blessed by my Father, take your inheritance, the kingdom prepared for you since the creation of the world." Mt 25:34 ". . . since you know that you will receive an inheritance from the Lord as a reward. It is the Lord Christ you are serving." Col 3:23-24

THE INTERCESSOR

Intercede (Webster's def.) Act or plead in behalf
Intercession (Bible dictionary def.) A plea on behalf of another

Intercession (praying for others) is a very important part of the Christian's responsibility toward others, believers and unbelievers alike.

So really, what is intercession? Is it just a thing of telling God what you desire for Him to do for others? Is it just bringing a list of requests before God, and trusting that He will answer in time?

Read Romans 15:30. "I urge you, brothers, by our Lord Jesus Christ and by the love of the Spirit, to **join me in my struggle** by praying to God for me."

This verse suggests putting ourselves in the other's place. Feeling what he or she is feeling, and praying from that angle. If the problem you were interceding about were your own, how fervently would you pray? How often would you pray about it? Would you cry out to God and may be even refuse to eat or rest till there is resolution? Would you hold on to God and refuse to let Him go till He has . . . . ? Jacob struggled with God all night till daybreak and said, "I will not let you go unless you bless me." Gen 32:26 And God blessed him, because he struggled with God and men and overcame. Gen 32:28

After all, we are supposed to love our neighbors as ourselves. By the same token, let us pray for others as we would pray for ourselves, putting in time, energy and faith. Although others might be praying about the same issue, let us pray as if the answers to those needs depended solely on our prayers. In other words, it should not be out of sight out of mind, praying about it once and forgetting about it. Let us remember our charge, "Carry each other's burdens, and in this way you will fulfill the law of Christ." Gal 6:2

Do unto others as you will have them do unto you, so pray for others as intensely as you would love to see them pray for you.

So as we see the weight people feel under their burdens, whether they remember to ask for our support or not, let us come along side of them and **join in their struggle by praying to God for them.**

MEMORIZE *"Peter was kept in prison, but the church was earnestly praying to God for him."* **Acts 12:5**

THE IMPORTANCE OF KNOWING GOD'S WORD

We do not have our Bibles with us every second of the day. However, there are many instances during the day when we need the ministry of the word. In such instances, the right verse will come to mind, if we previously knew it. So without a Bible in hand, we can still meditate on the word of God and apply it as needed.

DO YOU NEED ASSURANCE OF FORGIVENESS?

This verse will come in handy if you've previously commit it memory
"I write to you, dear children, because your sins have been forgiven on account of His name." 1 Jn 2:12

DOES THE DEVIL COME AT YOU WITH LIES AND ACCUSATIONS?

You could fight back, reminding him that he has been hurled down from heaven (defeated). Rev 12:10b Jesus did, He said to him: "It is written . . ." Mt 4:4 Luke 4:4

ARE YOU DEBATING IF YOU SHOULD OR SHOULDN'T FORGIVE SOMEONE?

You would know what to do if you knew this verse "For if you forgive men when they sin against you, your heavenly Father will also forgive you." Mt 6:14

WHICH KIND OF HUMAN COUNSEL IS BETTER?

If you knew Psalm 1, you will have the answer. "Blessed is the man who does not walk in the counsel of the wicked." Ps 1:1a

DO YOU NEED COMFORT?

If you knew this verse you could claim it, "Never will I leave you; never will I forsake you." Heb 13:5

DO YOU NEED TO SHARE WITH SOMEONE ELSE?

You cannot go wrong when you bring scripture to bear on an issue, you will not have to defend it. Let us study the word so we can confidently say: "The Bible says . . . ."

If you knew Romans 3:23-24, you can share it with someone who needs to know it, "for all have sinned and fall short of the glory of God, and are justified freely by His grace through the redemption that came by Christ Jesus."

MEMORY VERSE FOR THIS WEEK

"I have hidden your word in my heart that I might not sin against you." Ps 119:11

THE 'IFS' OF GOD'S PROMISES

The promises of God are for us, His children (those who believe on the name of Jesus Christ, the Son of God for forgiveness, salvation, and eternal life). He made these promises so we can know and remember His love, care, concern and provision for us. Sometimes, the fulfillment of some of the promises is based on conditions that we have to meet. It is very easy to claim the promises without satisfying the conditions. I strongly believe that God expects us to do our part to move His hand to do His part. The Scriptures tell us that God is no respecter of persons, and He does not show partiality. Therefore, I don't think He will make excuses for anyone. Any time we ignore the "if" in a promise we are essentially saying it is okay if the promise is unfulfilled.

Below are some of the 'if' promises:

+ "**If** my people who are called by name, will humble themselves, and pray and seek my face and turn away from their wicked ways, then will I hear from heaven and will forgive their sins and will heal their land." 2 Chr 7:14 This sounds like the solution to our world's sad condition. Sin is everywhere, and shows up in numerous forms. We all know about them, hear about them, comment about them, pray, and wish God will intervene. He said, He will hear, forgive our sins, and heal our land. How about that big 'if'? What are we expected to do to move God's hand to intervene? We, the children of God will have to humble ourselves, pray, seek His face, and turn away from our own wicked ways. This seems like a small price to pay to bring healing to our country and our world. This verse is calling Christians to repentance, to godly living,

222

and to intercession. If we take this seriously, we can trust God to turn our world around.

+ "If a man remains in me and I in him, he will bear much fruit; apart from me you can do nothing." Jn 15:5b Do we want to bear fruit to the glory of God? The only prescribed way is to remain in Christ, allowing Him to live His life through us.

+ "If you remain in me and my words remain in you, ask whatever you wish, and it will be given." Jn 15:7 If God's word abides in us, it will transform our minds, and our desires will line up with His plans for us. So our prayers will not be contrary to His will, and whatever we ask of Him will be in accordance to His will and He will grant it.

+ "You are my friends, if you do what I command you." Jn 15:14 There is an old chorus that goes like this, "The best friend to have is Jesus/x2, He will hear me when I call, He will keep me lest I fall, O, the best friend to have is Jesus." In order to be able to sing confidently about friendship with the Savior, we have to do what He commands. Friends fail, family fails, and society fails, but Jesus never fails. So let's treasure our friendship with Him and do whatever it takes to maintain it.

+ "If you obey my commands, you will remain in my love." Jn 15: 10a Disobeying God (sin) puts a separation between us and God, and robs us of joy and peace. If we desire an unbroken fellowship with Him, we have to be obedient. He prefers our obedience to sacrifices. In 1 Sam 15:23b He says, "To obey is better than sacrifice, and to heed is better than the fat of rams." After King David's sin of adultery and murder, he went through a period of spiritual loneliness. He cried out in desperation in Psalm 51. In verses 10 through 12, he said, "Create in me a pure heart, O God, and renew a steadfast Spirit within me. Do not cast me from your presence or take your Holy Spirit from me. Restore to me the joy of your salvation and grant a willing spirit, to sustain me." If we desire an enjoyable ongoing fellowship with the Lord, the key is obedience. The hymnist rightfully said, "Trust and obey, for there's no other way to be happy in Jesus, but to trust and obey."

+ Jesus promised to make the world know that we are His disciples, **if** we love one another. Jn 13:35 What will the world think if we tear each other down, refuse to forgive, and do not take care of each other? The world will probably think it is better off without God and the Church. If we want the world to know we are His followers, His children, and His servants, we have to take care of each other. In 1 Cor 13:4-8a, He tells us what love is. If we allow the Lord to love others through us the way He teaches us, the world will want what we have.

If we earnestly want God's promises fulfilled, let us do our part.

THE FEAR OF THE LORD

The fear (reverence) of the Lord **should:**

Make us wise "The fear of the Lord is the beginning of knowledge." Prov 1:7
and knowledgeable
"The fear of the Lord—that is wisdom, and to shun evil is understanding." Jb 28:28
"The fear of the Lord is the beginning of wisdom; all who follow His precepts have good understanding." Ps 111:10

Make us hate evil "To fear the Lord is to hate evil" Prov 8:13

Make us obedient "And now, O Israel, what does the Lord your God ask of you but to fear the Lord your God, to walk in all His ways, to love Him, to serve the Lord your God with all your heart and with all your soul, and to observe the Lord's commands and decrees that I am giving you today for your own good." Deu 10:12

"If you fear the Lord and serve and obey Him and do not rebel against His commands, . . . 1Sam 12:14

Make us worship (this is a hymn)
O, worship the Lord in the beauty of holiness! Bow down before Him,
His glory proclaim; With gold of obedience and incense of lowliness,
Kneel and adore Him, The Lord is His name.

Make us fulfill our duty ". . . here is the conclusion of the matter: Fear God and keep His commandments, for this is the <u>whole duty of man</u>." Ecc 12:13

REWARDS OF GODLY FEAR

"How great is <u>your goodness</u>, which you have stored up for those who fear you" Ps 31:19

"Who, then, is the man that fears the Lord? He <u>will instruct him</u> in the way chosen for him. <u>He will spend his days in prosperity</u>, and <u>his descendants will inherit the land</u>." Ps 25:12-13

"As a father has compassion on his children, so the Lord has <u>compassion</u> on those who fear Him" Ps 103:13

"The Lord <u>delights</u> in those who fear Him, who put their hope in His unfailing love" Ps147:11

"The Lord <u>confides</u> in those who fear Him; He makes His covenant known to them."
Ps 25:14

"The fear of the Lord <u>adds length to life</u>, but the years of the wicked are cut short." Prov 10:27

THE FAMILY OF GOD

Webster defines family as

+ Parents and their children
+ Relatives

It is therefore safe to say the family of God is God and us His children. How do we each function in our natural families? To some extent there are minor differences, but basically family members love, give and spend time together. Families get together for meals, entertainment, celebrations of occasion that call for celebration.

The spiritual family should function in the same way, and for the most part we do. However, some don't make spending time with the family a priority. Simply put, some don't go to church, and others go very infrequently. The word admonishes us this way, "Let us not give up meeting together, as some are in the habit of doing, but let us encourage one another—and all the more as you see the day approaching." Heb 10:25

Is the day approaching? I think so! That's the more reason we should spend time together in the word and in prayer. Where else can we find great fellowship and clean fun? David said, "I was glad when they said unto me, 'let us go into the house of the Lord'." Ps 122:1

The devil will always suggest reasons why we shouldn't go. Some of the reasons can be, "you are too tired today." "You are already late." "You have nothing to wear." "Your friends aren't going today." Etc. The devil's goal is for us to displease God, thereby depriving us of His fellowship (If I regard iniquity in my heart, the Lord will not hear).

The early Church (read the book of Acts) was always meeting to pray and break bread. They did not practice individual Christianity even though they spent time in prayer and study alone. (Peter on the roof in the house of Simon the tanner in Acts 10:9). We need to remind ourselves that there is power in united prayer for, "If two of you on earth agree about anything you ask for, it will be done for you of my Father in heaven. For where two or three come together in my name, there I am with them." Mt 18:19-20

If two or three people praying together can make a difference, can you imagine the difference praying congregations are making? Amazing!

We need to have a one on one time with God, but also a corporate time with Him and other believers. The family needs to get together, often.

Sharing our joys, trials and understanding of the word builds us up, and builds up others as well. The Psalmist was very good at doing this; he loved declaring the love of God in the congregation of the righteous. He says, "Praise the Lord. I will extol the Lord with all my heart in the council of the upright and in the assembly. Ps 111:1

"Let them exalt Him in the assembly of the people and praise Him in the council of the elders." Ps 107:32

Going to Church, fellowship meetings etc. should be a priority. Let's not fall into the devil's trap. Like the Psalmist, let's rejoice at the opportunity to be in the house of the Lord. Believers in parts of the world where there is hostility against the Church would love to have this opportunity to fellowship without hindrance.

THE EVIDENCE

There is a tree in a neighbor's front yard. What drew my attention to it the first time I saw it, was its beautiful foliage. Of course I had no idea what kind of tree it was. With my limited horticultural knowledge I was unable to guess. However, given time, it became evident that it was an apple tree.

How did I figure it out? The Scriptures clearly teaches, "By their fruits you will know them." Mt 7:16

As soon as that tree started to bear apples, I concluded it was an apple tree. I was very sure about my conclusion because trees do not bear anything else besides what they were made to bear.

So if you never open your mouth to say you are a child of God (which you should), would people looking at your way of life be able to conclude that you are a Christian? In other words, as I've heard someone say before, "if Christianity were a crime, would there be enough evidence to convict you?

We cannot fake Christianity, but as Christians, we should allow the Spirit to renew our minds through the word, and to live through us. We can then agree with the Apostle Paul when he says, "I have been crucified with Christ and I no longer live, but Christ lives in me." Gal 2:20a

Having a renewed mind is to allow the spirit to pattern our minds after Christ's.

Apples can be good or bad; sometimes they are worm infested, very watery, mushy, or very sweet and crunchy. Other times they fall off the tree before they are matured enough for human consumption.

By the same token, as Christians we can exhibit fruits that are less than desirable. However, if we abide in Christ who is the Vine, (we are the branches) God prunes and nourishes us enabling us to bear good quality fruit. According to Jesus' word in Jn 15, God cuts off every branch that does not bear fruit. (I am not quite sure how, but I think we should be concerned.) Are you a Christian, consistently or just sometimes, when it's convenient for you?

A fruit from one branch may not be as good as one from another branch depending on their level of maturity, but we need to make sure we are constantly abiding in Jesus, the Vine. That is the only way to guarantee our ability to mature and bear fruits (Love, joy, peace, patience, kindness, goodness, faithfulness, gentleness, self-control. Gal 5:22-23a) that convince the world we are of God.

MEMORIZE: "I am the true vine, and my Father is the gardener. He cuts off every branch in me that bears no fruit, while every branch that does bear fruit he prunes so that it will be even more fruitful." Jn 15:1-2

THE DISTINGUISHING MARKS

There are characteristics that tell us more about a person or a thing. If you go into a doctor's office, without seeing anybody, and you hear a baby cry you can tell there is a baby somewhere in that office. If you go into a neighbor's house without knowing she has a phone, if you hear one ring you can safely assume she has a phone.

In the same way, it should be obvious to us and others when the power of God is at work in us proving His presence. Many years ago, Moses had a very interesting dialogue with God, recorded in Exodus 33:12-16

Moses wanted assurance from God that He'd be amongst them when they journeyed to the Promised Land. He asked two questions that would help God understand the importance of His presence on this trip. (Not that God needed this lesson)

The first question was, "How will anyone know that you are pleased with me and with your people unless you go with us?" v 16a

The second question, "What else will distinguish me and your people from all the other people on the face of the earth?" v 16b

I love these questions, especially the second one, because it tells me the importance of allowing my life to prove the power and presence of God in my life. Christians and unbelievers alike have problems and needs, but how the Christian handles and resolves his or her issues should be very different from how the unbeliever handles his or hers. How do we handle crisis, poor health, frustration, business, financial loss or anything else? If God is with us we should be able to exhibit calmness and strength through His power and prayer, because we can do all things through Christ who strengthens us. Php 4:13

This is not implying that crises are fun, because they are not, and the devil makes sure of that. Instead, it is saying we do not need not panic and worry like the unbeliever; our response should be honoring to God.

God made Moses a promise in Ex 34:10b, "I am making a covenant with you. Before all your people I will do wonders never before done in any nation in all the world. **The people you live among will see** how awesome is the work that I, the Lord, will do for you." We can also look back to the Israelites' deliverance from Egypt; none of the plagues affected them even though they lived in that land. We all know it was the hand of God protecting them.

EZEKIEL'S UNUSUAL FIELDTRIP

God took the prophet Ezekiel on a fieldtrip to a valley full of human bones. He made Ezekiel walk back and forth among the bones to give him plenty of time to make some good observations. After the tour of the valley, God asked him, "Son of man, can these bones live?" Eze 37:3a

God knew the answer to His own question of course. This brings to mind, the account of the feeding of the 5,000 in John 6. When Jesus saw the great crowd, He asked Phillip, "Where shall we buy bread for these people to eat?" Jn 6:5b The passage goes on to explain that Jesus asked the question only to test Phillip, for He already had in mind what He was going to do. So God already knew the bones could come back to life.

Ezekiel's observation and assessment of the situation:

1. There were **many** bones, scattered
2. The bones were **very** dry (indicative of lifelessness)

If Ezekiel had been talking with a fellow man, his answer to the question would have been, "Certainly not." But since he believed in the power of God, he answered differently, "O Sovereign Lord, you alone know." Eze 37:3b In essence, Ezekiel was saying, "Humanly speaking, 'No.' but with you God, all things are possible."

Sometimes, we face situations that are humanly hopeless, because they seem to have no explanations, no answers or solutions and no way out of them. Are you going through something like that right now? Do you think it can get better, or have you already given up hope? First, God wants us to realize and admit that our situations are hopeless without Him, just like Ezekiel admitted the hopelessness of the situation in the valley. Secondly, He wants us to understand and confess to Him that, without Him we can do nothing.

Jn 15:5b

Once Ezekiel acknowledged God's power, God proceeded to put His plan into action. He had Ezekiel prophesy to the bones, "I will make breath enter you, and you will come to life. I will attach tendons to you and make flesh come upon you and cover you with skin; I will put breath in you, and you will come to life. Then you will know that I am the Lord." Eze 37:6

After the prophecy, the miracle began to happen, one step at a time. Matching bones came together to form the skeletons, (the body frame). Then came tendons and flesh to hold them together and skin to cover them. To complete the miracle, breath entered them and they came to life. Amen!

God can mend all situations, but if He doesn't, it's for a reason. Instead, He gives us grace to bear so that in the end He gets the glory. "My grace is sufficient for you, for my strength is made perfect in weakness." 2 Cor 12:9

God desires to demonstrate His power through us, either through the miracle of deliverance or the miracle of grace to bear.

"Can these bones live?" The answer is yes, if the Lord so desires! A leper once said to Jesus, "Lord, if you are willing, you can make me clean." Mt 8:2b

Jesus' ability has never been in question. However, we can't always be sure of His willingness because His plans might be totally different from what we ask, and even though He could do it, doing it will change the bigger picture. This knowledge shouldn't stop us from asking; we just need to ask in faith according to His will. Paul believed God could heal him of whatever he had, and that's why, three times he prayed to have it removed. 2 Cor 12:8

God of course decided to give him grace to bear rather than heal him. V9

Jesus prayed in Gethsemane, "Yet not as I will, but as you will." Mt 26:39b If God had aborted the crucifixion in answer to Jesus' prayer, our fellowship with God would not have been restored, and we'll definitely be on our way to hell.

We need to always come to God in faith, allowing Him to reveal His will and plans for us. Knowing that His plans will always be for our welfare. Jer 29:11

Memorize—"Son of man, can these bones live?" Ezek 37:3a

WHAT IS EVIL

The Bible says, "To fear of the Lord is to hate evil." Prov 8:13a In order to hate evil we first have to define the word 'evil'. So what is evil?

EVIL wickedness; slanderous or injurious actions (dictionary definition)
WICKED evil, sinful

Some reference to evil
For they cannot sleep till they do evil; they are robbed of slumber till they make someone fall" Prov 4:16
"Woe to those who call evil good and good evil" Isa 5:20

HOW TO HATE EVIL IN ONE'S SELF

Admit it "I have sinned against the Lord." 2 Sam 12:13 (David said to Nathan)

Call it by name: (don't take it lightly, God doesn't) "For I know my transgressions, and my sin is always before me." Ps51:3

Repent Ps 51

Don't make excuses for yourself "The woman you put here with me—she gave some fruit from the tree, and I ate it." Gen 3: 12 (Adam's excuse for disobeying God)

Ask for forgiveness, and strength to overcome "Wash away all my iniquity and cleanse me from my sin." Ps 51: 2 (read all of Ps 51, that's David after adultery with Bathsheba)

Ask others to hold you accountable "Therefore confess your sins to each other and pray for each other so that you may be healed. The prayer of a righteous man is powerful and effective." James 5:16

Avoid situations that foster evil "From the roof he saw a woman bathing" 2 Sam 11:2 Then David sent messengers to get her." 2 Sam 11:4

HATING and REBUKING EVIL IN OTHERS

Do not condone: Sapphira agreed with her husband, Ananias to lie to the apostles about the proceeds from the sale of their property. Peter questioned her after Ananias had told the lie. "Tell me, is this the price you and Ananias got for the land?" Yes, she said, that is the price." Acts 5:8 (That was a lie, Peter called it lying to God, not to men. Read the story in Acts 5:1-11).

"When you see a thief, you join with him; you throw in your lot with adulterers . . . you speak continually against your brother . . . . you thought I was altogether like you"
Ps 50 18-21a
"It is actually reported that there is sexual immorality among you . . . . shouldn't you rather be filled with grief?" 1 Cor 5:1-3

DISAGREEING WITH GOD!!

There are many people out there who disagree with what the Bible says. For one thing, they don't believe the Bible is the word of God. They argue it was written by men, and hence don't feel obligated to obey what it says. The truth is, although God used men, "No prophecy of Scripture came about by the prophet's own interpretation. For prophecy never had its origin in the will of man, but men spoke from God as they were carried along by the Holy Spirit." 2 Pet 1:20b-21

Now in our society, we hear this statement a lot, "Everyone is entitled to their own opinion." Whereas that statement is primarily true because it is a free country, it fails to address the implication of that way of thinking. If one is free to believe whatever one wants, then one should also know and gladly accept the consequences of what one believes.

Disagreeing with what the Bible says does not change anything it says or how it is supposed to apply. According to Ezekiel 18:4b for example, "The soul who sins is the one who will die," so if someone refuses to believe that statement does God excuse him on the basis that he did not believe it? I don't think so. How about, "For the wages of sin is death, but the gift of God is eternal life in Christ Jesus our Lord."? Rom 6:23

For the person who chooses to have nothing to do with the Bible or believes only parts of it, does God let him go free because he chose not to believe it? Absolutely not!!

As much as people have the right to believe what they want, God also has the right and duty to stay faithful to His word. So they can choose to disregard the Bible, and God also can and will painfully choose to condemn them to hell. I say painfully because

God really doesn't want any in hell. He wants all men to be saved and to come to the knowledge of the truth. 1 Tim 2:4

However, people have to want what God wants for them. They have to ask for salvation.

Again, in 1 Pet 3:9b He emphasizes His desire for all men to be saved. "He is patient with you, not wanting anyone to perish, but everyone to come to repentance."

Hell was originally prepared for the devil and his demons, but for God to remain who He is, faithful and just, He will have to send unbelievers to hell as well. "Then He will say to those on His left, 'Depart from me, you who are cursed, into the eternal fire prepared for the devil and his angels.'" Mt 25:41.

Arrogantly ignoring the claims of the Bible does not hurt God; it hurts only those who ignore it, because whether they believe it or not, someday they will be judged by it. They will someday, at the name Jesus, bow their knee and confess to God.

We therefore, have a responsibility to pray and witness to as many as the Lord brings our way. Time is short and many continue to be arrogant, not understanding the consequences of their behavior. Soon it will be too late to make a difference!!

IN THE DESERT, VALLEY OR DESERTED ISLAND

The desert, valley and deserted islands are not habitable places. People do not make such places their home, and if they find themselves there, it is always a temporary situation; they are just passing through.

The desert is a dry, hot place, water is scarce, food is scarce, and nobody lives there. A person who lives in a desert will feel very lonely, isolated, hungry and thirsty. Should he be in trouble, there will be no help. Nobody in their right mind will choose to make a desert their home. Therefore anybody in a desert was most likely placed there, intentionally, by another or got there because he or she got lost.

The Israelites were in the desert not by choice. God was taking them through the desert to the Promised Land, a place flowing with milk and honey. They could have made that journey, by-passing the desert, but God had a good reason for taking them through the wilderness. Ex 13:17 They were excited about the Promised Land alright, but they hated their desert experiences so much so they wished they were back in Egypt, as slaves. They were willing to do anything to be out of the desert, including killing Moses, their leader. They had no food, God sent them manna; they had no meat, God sent them quails. Ex 16. They had no water God sent them water from the Rock! Ex 17:1-6

We all have trials in our lives we can refer to as deserts, valleys or deserted islands. Life in our individual deserts is dry, painful, exhausting and quite often unexplainable, with no end in sight. How did we get there? Where were we going? How are we coping?

So how did we get there? Most likely, God put us there or allowed our circumstances to work out that way, so He can have us to Himself in the desert. He needs to get our undivided attention and teach us lessons we cannot learn otherwise. Jer 29:11

And where were we going? We might not know the short term destination but the final destination is to be like Christ. He is teaching us lessons to mature us and make us fit for heaven. Ja 1:2-4

How are we coping? We should be looking to Christ the author and finisher of our faith. Heb 12:1b-2 Focusing on the goal will make the desert more tolerable and hopefully we will even get to appreciate it. I am not sure the Israelites ever got to the point of appreciating their desert experiences as a nation, but we need to. I know of individuals who are thankful for past painful experiences, because of the lasting lessons they learned to benefit themselves and others.

Let's learn from the Israelites. Because of their rebellion and murmuring in the wilderness, they stayed there longer than they would have. The older generation, including Moses, did not make it into the Promised Land. We need to get with God's program. We need to make it safely through the desert into the Promised Land. "Weeping may remain for a night, but rejoicing comes in the morning." Ps 30:5b

CHOSEN FOR A PURPOSE

"Chosen" is defined as having been selected as the best or most appropriate. 'Being chosen' always conveys the idea that some were better qualified than others. This definition doesn't fit the Christian's definition at all, because when God chose us, he did not compare us to anyone else. He did not think we were better than others or the best of the lot. In fact, had He made comparisons, the thief on the cross would not have had a chance; he was a murderer. I wouldn't have had a chance, and you wouldn't have had a chance either. "For **all** have sinned and fall short of the glory of God." Rom 3:23

How about Paul (AKA Saul), he persecuted the Church terribly. What did he say of himself? He said, "I persecuted the followers of this way (Christianity) to their death, arresting both men and women and throwing them into prison . . ." Acts 22: 4-5 Later on, as an apostle he said, "For I am the least of the apostles and do not deserve to be called an apostle, because I persecuted the Church of God." 1 Cor 15:9 To be chosen therefore is by grace only, not by being better, the most deserving, or the most qualified.

As Christians, God chose us; we did not choose Him. Jn 15: 16a He chose us not because of any good thing we have done but because of His love and mercy. In fact, He chose us while we were still sinners, going our own way and doing our own thing, with no regard for Him at all. Rom 5:8 He chose us out of the world, (Jn 15:19b), and Peter says to us, "You are a chosen people, a royal priesthood, a holy nation, a people belonging to God." 1 Peter 2:9a

God chose us for a reason. We have a mandate, a purpose to fulfill. Jesus said to His friends, "I chose you to **go and bear fruit-**

fruit that will last." Jn 15:16b Paul the apostle tells us in Eph 1:4 that God chose us in Him before the creation of the world to **be holy and blameless in His sight.** How do we get to be holy and blameless? We get to be holy by living godly lives, walking as He walked, i.e. in His footsteps. 2 Pet 3:11 Also in Eph 1:12b, he says we are called for the **praise of Christ's glory.** "Let your light so shine before men that they may see your good works, glorify your Father which is in heaven." Again, Peter tells us in 1 Peter 2:9b that the reason we are called is to **declare the praises of Him who called us out of darkness into His marvelous light.** "I will extol the Lord at all times; His praise will always be on my lips." Ps 34:1 How well are we doing in fulfilling our call? What kind o fruits are we bearing? "But the fruit of the Spirit is love, joy, peace, patience, kindness, goodness, faithfulness, gentleness and self-control. Against such things there is no law." Gal 5:22-23. In order for our fruits to last, the bearing has to be ongoing, because when we stop bearing fruits, we lose what we already have.

This is my prayer for us: **Lord, please show us how to live in order to make you attractive to the world, and to each other.**

JONAH, WHAT WAS HE THINKING?

God asked Jonah to go and preach repentance to the Ninevites. "Go to the great city of Nineveh and preach against it, because its wickedness has come up before me." Jonah 1:2

Jonah thought to himself, "No way! Knowing God, He will forgive them and not destroy them, if they repent, (Jonah 4:2b) and I'll look foolish. I know what I'll do; I'll go as far away from Nineveh as I can possibly go. I'll get on the next available ship and I'll not have to carry out this assignment." God must have smiled!

Jonah implemented his plan and got on the next available ship, Tarshish-bound. After paying the fare, he went to the lower deck and went to sleep. It wasn't long before things got rough at sea. All efforts to save the ship and sailors failed. Everyone started calling on their god for deliverance; Jonah of course was fast asleep. When they awakened him, he admitted he was the cause of the storm. "Why?" They asked him. "He was running away from the Lord." Jonah 1:10

This brings me to my question, "What was Jonah thinking?" Did he really think he could get away from God? He apparently thought so, since he did run. The Psalmist says, "Where can I go from your Spirit? Where can I flee from your presence? If I go up to the heavens, you are there; if I make my bed in the depths, you are there. If I rise on the wings of the dawn, if I settle on the far side of the sea, even there your hand will guide me; your right hand will hold me fast. If I say, 'surely the darkness will hide me and the light become night around me,' even the darkness will not be dark to you; the night will shine like the day, for darkness is as light to you." Ps 139:7-12

So we see the futility of running from God. He is everywhere! In fact He is the one who guides us to where we go, making sure we are safe. He knows our plans before we device and implement them, "O Lord, you have searched me and you know me. You know when I sit and when I rise; you perceive my thoughts from afar. You discern my going out and my lying down; you are familiar with all my ways. Before a word is on my tongue you know it completely, O Lord." Ps 139:1-4

My friend, are you running or trying to hide from God? Why? Are you running from some assignment or because of some sin you've committed? In which direction are you running, and what is your desired destination? Can you think of any place you can hide where God might not be able to find you? Let me assure you; there is no such place in heaven or earth, so stop running and stop trying to hide. Surrender to Him and let Him enable you to do His bidding.

Although Jonah had thought he could run from God, he soon woke up to the realization that God sees and hears us no matter where we are. He prayed from the belly of the fish. God answered his prayer, proof that He is never far from us. "And the Lord commanded the fish, and it vomited Jonah onto dry land." Jonah 2:10

LOVING THE BRETHREN

WHO IS THE BRETHREN? (Christians, the church, the body of Christ)

<u>DISCIPLE</u>—a follower, particularly one who follows Jesus Christ (dictionary def).

"And the disciples were called Christians first in Antioch." Acts 11:26b

Therefore Christian=Disciple of Christ

WHY SHOULD WE LOVE THE BRETHREN?

Jesus commanded it, and it is proof of discipleship
"A new command I give you: Love one another. <u>As I have loved you</u>, so you must love one another. By this all men will know that you are my disciples, if you love one another." Acts 13:35-36
"My command is this: Love each other <u>as I have loved you</u>." Jn 15:12

HOW SHOULD WE LOVE? (as Christ loved us)

<u>SINCERILY</u>—"Love must be sincere; . . . . be devoted to one another in brotherly love. Honor one another above yourselves." Ro 12:9-10

<u>ABOUNDING</u> . . . . "May the Lord make your love increase and overflow for each other and for everyone else, just as ours does for you." 1 Thes 3:12

DEEPLY . . ."... Love one another deeply from the heart." 1Pet 1:22b
"God can testify how I long for all of you with the affection of Jesus Christ." Phil 1:8

RESULTS OF BROTHERLY LOVE

1. God is glorified "This is to my Father's glory, that you bear much fruit, showing yourselves to be my Disciples." Jn 15:8
2. Our friendship with Christ is confirmed "You are my friends if you do what I command you." Jn 15:14
3. The needs of the body are met because we pray, give and support each other as needed.

"Let us not love with words or tongue but with actions and in truth." 1Jn 3:18 (read11-19)

MEMORY VERSE "Whoever does not love, does not know God, because God is love." 1 Jn 4:8

This week, quietly before the Lord, let us individually try to answer these questions:

1. How has Christ loved me? (We have to know how, because He wants us to love as He loved us).
2. How can I show love to my brethren? (When we find out, let's put it into action).

GOD'S GRACE

Three weeks of terror just ended
Two men terrorized numerous neighborhoods
Wounds were physical, emotional, mental and deep
Fear crossed all boundaries, age, gender, race, nationality, profession
Three weeks of terror just ended

Three weeks of terror just ended
Many lost their lives
Some lost body parts, enduring unbelievable pain
Many more lost loved ones; spouses, parents, children and friends
Three weeks of terror just ended

Three weeks of terror just ended
Those who'd rather not leave home are venturing out again
Those who zigzagged in the parking lots are walking straight lines again
School and work attendance is back to normal
Three weeks of terror just ended

Three weeks of terror just ended
Children are playing in the backyards and streets again
Window shades and curtains are up once again
Three weeks of terror just ended

Three weeks of terror just ended
Probably, anyone who lost a loved one is asking, "why me?"
It could have happened to me or my loved ones, but it didn't

All because of your grace
Why did I deserve your grace more than the others?
Three weeks of terror just ended

Three weeks of terror just ended
You love the victims as much as the spared ones
No one understands why they perished, but you do
For your thoughts and ways are higher than ours
Three weeks of unexcused terror just ended

For the dead who loved you, we know are at rest
For their loving survivors, please grant grace and strength to go
on
When grieving is over, may they look back and see the good you
intended
May they be able to comfort others with the comfort they received
from you
Three weeks of terror just ended and your grace has been
sufficient.

AT THE TRAFFIC LIGHTS OF LIFE

Our journey through this life is like being on a highway, and taking our cue from the different color traffic lights. We are always at one of three lights. We are either at a stop (red), getting ready to stop (yellow), or in motion (green). The color changes determine how long we are supposed to stay at each light. In order to ensure our safety and the safety of other travelers, we cannot ignore any of the indicators for change.

If we stand still at a green light, travelling time is prolonged, we arrive late at our destination, and we delay other travelers, and can potentially be the cause of an accident. If we choose to stay in motion when the light is red, we run the risk of accidents, getting hurt and or hurting other travelers, be it pedestrians or other drivers. If we try to avoid the red light by rushing through the yellow light, we risk going through the red light, and possibly causing an accident. We need to respond to each color traffic light appropriately and in a timely manner. In order to do that, we need to be alert and watchful so we don't miss any of the prompts.

When God gives the signal to move (green), we need to move prayerfully and in faith trusting that He knows where He is leading, even when we are not sure. Moses didn't know the solution to, "Tell the Israelites to move on." Ex 14:15b, when he and the Israelites were sandwiched between the Red sea in front and the Egyptian soldiers behind. Have you taken matching orders not knowing where you are headed? If your orders came from the Father, you don't have to worry; He has it all under control. Let us be on our guard so that we don't miss any orders for change when He issues them.

Please let's not speed up when God says, "Slow down" (yellow light). Speeding up to escape or shorten pain and suffering won't accomplish God's purposes for us. God through Joshua, commanded the Israelites to match around Jericho once a day for six days, then seven times on the seventh day (Jos 6:3-5). They could have decided to speed up things by walking two or more times per day or marched thirteen times the first day to get the job completed sooner than later, but they didn't. God had a good reason for this seemingly strange military strategy; the Israelites didn't have to know the reason why, all they needed to do was obey. Had they not followed His orders to the later, the outcome could have been very different, most likely not in their favor.

Then, there comes the most dreaded time when God says, "Wait!" Waiting is not easy, especially when we don't know what's supposed to happen next; we can get restless, tired, inpatient, and whinny. But charging ahead of God always messes things up. Let us wait! During that waiting period, we need to exercise patience, faith, and be prayerful, and expectant. Sometime after Jesus' resurrection, before His ascension, He gave the apostles this command, "Do not leave Jerusalem, but wait for the gift my Father promised, which you have heard me speak about." Acts 1:4 That gift was the Holy Spirit! When He came, He filled them with power to be His witnesses. They were no longer afraid of the authorities; they preached with boldness in His name and healed the sick in His name. Had they not waited expectantly, patiently, and prayerfully, the outcome might have been different.

The toughest part of knowing which light we've come to is the ability to hear God's voice distinctly. We definitely cannot heed God's direction, if we cannot hear Him, and we don't hear Him because we don't wait on Him enough to hear Him speak to us. We are always on a move, in a rush, and our minds wonder, and our enemy, the devil likes it that way. In Revelation 1:10, John who had been banished to the Island of Patmos because of his faith says, "On the Lord's Day, I was in the Spirit, and I heard . . ." In order to hear the Lord's voice we need to be prayerful.

STOP HANGING AND START RESTING

'Hanging in there' has become the response to a friendly "How are you?" What do we mean when we say "I am hanging in there"? I think it means, things are not exactly what they should be, but we are waiting to see how they turn out. I am trying to get away from saying that because I don't like the imagery I get from "hanging in". It is like hanging from a tree limb, suspended between the sky and earth.

Hanging from a tree limb appears very uncomfortable, and does not appear to offer any hope of rescue or assurance of when help might arrive. When one is hanging, there is the possibility of letting go when one gets exhausted, and what a painful crash that could ensue. There is also the possibility of the tree limb giving way under the hanging weight and becoming detached. Again, the resulting crash could be very painful.

A better response I believe should be, "I am resting in the Lord." This will convey the idea that although one is tired, one is resting safely in the Lord's arms. When we are in the Lord's arms, there is no possibility of falling, because He is an immovable Rock. The imagery of resting in the Lord is far more comforting than the imagery of hanging.

Psalm 55:22 says, "Cast your cares on the Lord, and He will sustain you; He will never let the righteous fall." The fact that God will sustain us should bring us comfort. Again, in 1 Peter 5:7, we are admonished to cast all our anxiety on the Lord because He cares for us. Casting our cares on the Lord means, we literally drop our cares, anxieties, etc. in his lap, sit back and trustingly watch Him tackle them all. When we drop a load in His lap, we no longer have it, and should therefore not feel the pressure of it; we should feel light and free.

Having said that, let's ask ourselves, "Why do we sometimes go back to worrying about things we've dropped in His lap?" I think two of the reasons have to do with timing and the fear of the unknown. When we have a need, we come to the Lord with the attitude of an impatient toddler, the attitude of 'NOW'. So when it doesn't happen NOW, we take back our load. The other reason is, the 'HOW?' We wonder if He would do things exactly the way we desire of Him or if He would do it some other way. So again, being uncertain, we pick up our load, and off we go because we disagree with how He might solve the problem.

When we reclaim our loads we have no idea what the outcome would be, and that is how we arrive at "hanging in there", which is not a very good place to be. May God help us to leave the timing and the how in His hands, so we can rest comfortably in Him.

A SONG IN THE NIGHT

Some synonyms for nighttime are: hours of darkness, dark, and darkness. Sometimes we refer to life's difficulties as nighttime, and look forward to daytime when things will be different. What do we do during the waiting time? The easiest is worry, even though we know and tell ourselves we should be praying. Some are even depressed, short-tempered, and withdrawn.

Paul and Silas took a different path. They had been jailed for preaching the gospel, and during the night when they could have laid awake and worried, they sang praises to God. They could have wondered what their fate was going to be in the morning, how they could get out of their situation, and on, and on. Instead, they praised God, knowing that He knew all about their situation and knew how to rescue them, and how to bring good out of that situation.

How did they get to be in jail? They were not committing a crime, they were doing what they believed was right. In fact they were minding their own business. They had just cast out a demon from a slave girl who was making money for her owners by fortune telling. Needless to say the owners were unhappy when they lost their source of income. Consequently, they were brought before the magistrate who had them thrown into prison.

Are you struggling with a situation (darkness) in your life that was not the result of anything you've done wrong? What are you doing about it? Are you trying to justify yourself, thinking how unfair life has been to you? Are you going to pray and sing in the midst of your trouble? The apostle Paul knew from experience the benefits of giving thanks in all circumstances, including dark ones. Rom 8:28

What was the result of their jail experience? God intervened! There was a violent earthquake, violent enough to shake the foundations of the prison, fly the prison doors open, and loosen every prisoner's chains. Paul and Silas did not know how, when or if God was going to intervene, but they trusted Him to work it all out. Like the three Jewish boys in Babylon, God's deliverance or intervention was not the basis of their decisions to praise. Can you and I just trust God with our problems in an attitude of praise? If we postpone praise until the night is past, we might not be praising any time soon, because with God a day is like a thousand and a thousand like a day.

Through that experience the jailer and all his family became Christians. So all things did work out for good . . ." People were saved; Paul and Silas experienced God's faithfulness all over again. The Bible doesn't name the song they were singing, and I don't think it makes any difference. The most important thing is that they were praying and singing hymns to God. Their night didn't stop them from singing. How about you and how about me?

SECTION THREE:
SPECIAL DAYS

THANKSGIVING

On the first thanksgiving, the pilgrims were truly thankful for what God had done for them in their new homeland (USA). He had protected them from harsh weather, hostile neighbors and diseases, and given them a good harvest.

Later, 'Thanksgiving' was established as a National Holiday by President Abraham Lincoln during the American Civil War. In the proclamation President Lincoln specified that the last Thursday of each November should be set aside as a day to give thanks for the founding of our nation.

The fourth Thursday of each November therefore became a National Holiday; a day for 'Thanksgiving.' The celebration is usually marked with lots of cooking, get-togethers and feasting

What is our take on this celebration? Are we truly thankful, and for what? Do we focus on God in any way? Getting together with friends and family is great idea, but let us not forget the genesis of it, 'THANKFLNESS TO GOD'

There is so much we need to thank God for, not only on the last Thursday of every November but every moment, every day, and every night. God loves grateful people. He loves to be acknowledged and appreciated. After He cleansed the ten lepers, only one came back to say thanks. Jesus' response, "Were not all ten cleansed? Where are the other nine?" Lk 17:17 (They probably were off celebrating)

Think! Are you forgetting to say thanks for something? It's not too late to say it.

What are some of the things we need to be thankful for?

- The fact that we are here
- Health, daily provisions, accommodation,
- Gift of salvation
- The Word to help us grow
- The Spirit to comfort, lead and teach us
- Those who minister to us faithfully through preaching, teaching, music
- Freedom to worship
- Friends, family
- Jobs
- Things that bring us joy and laughter (like children and grand children)
- Those who pray for us and encourage us
- Technology (has enhanced our lives in so many ways)
- Advances in medicine
- The seasons and the beauty we see around us
- Governments and leaders who establish and enforce laws that protect us
- And so much more!

The Psalmist says,

"Give thanks to the Lord, for He is good; His love endures forever." Ps 118:1

"**Give thanks to the Lord**, call on His name; **make known** among the nations what He has done." Ps 105:1

"Give thanks to the Lord, for He is good; His love endures forever. Let the redeemed of the Lord (that's us) say this." Ps 107:1-2a

"Let them give thanks to the Lord for His unfailing love and His wonderful deeds for men." Ps 107:15

CELEBRATING JESUS

It's amazing how time flies. Christmas seems to be coming faster and faster each year. The planning, preparation, and anticipation make it a very exciting time, but, let us not forget who we celebrate. Christmas is all about Jesus even though some would like to see Him off the scene. Referring to this time of year as the 'holidays' does not change anything; it is still Christmas, Jesus' birthday.

If we are going to celebrate it, let's celebrate it for what it really is, because history cannot be changed or re-written. When He was born, God sent angels to announce to the shepherds, "A Savior is born." He has come to save mankind from sin. Herod, king in those days tried to get rid of Him but failed. How can humans get rid of God, the creator of the universe? Impossible!

People think refusing to accept the claims of Jesus as Savior excuses them from the penalty of sin. In fact, it doesn't. God is God, and has set things up the way they are for a reason. Those who disagree are not really doing themselves or anyone else any favors. God is not going to bend or change His rules because someone has reservations or disagreements.

So as we celebrate this season, year after year, let's remember, 'No Jesus, No Christmas'

He desires to have a personal relationship with each individual, but will not force His way into anyone's life. He has done His part by coming and dying to pay the penalty for our sin, past, present and future. We have to do our part by accepting the salvation He is offering so freely through faith in Him.

As we give and receive gifts, let's remember, God was the first one to give a gift, Jesus His Son. The Son gave His life and said, "I am the way, the truth and the life. No man comes to the Father except through me." "I am come that they might have life and have it to the fullest." This is Christmas!!

TIME TO CELEBRATE

Merchants startcelebrating Christmas months before the actual day. They do so not because they necessarily care anything about Jesus. I am sure many of these busy merchants do not believe in Him and probably have no idea what the celebration is all about. They most likely think, "It is the season to make the most money."

Aside from the merchants, a large percentage of the population makes preparations to celebrate Christmas. There is lots of buying, gift wrapping, giving and receiving. And O, let's not forget the Christmas trees and decorations and parties. Some people get so drunk; they don't remember any of it by the next day. Others get physically sick from all the eating and drinking; to them, that is Christmas.

Christmas has become the busiest most stressful time of the year. I doubt that it will ever change. However, if we allow Jesus to remain the focus of all the activities as He should, there will be reduction in stress. The unbelievers do not know what is appropriate for the season; hence it is up to us, Christians to lead the way, putting Christ back into Christmas.

What do you do Christmas after Christmas? How do you celebrate? Do you give any presents? As you give, especially to the unbeliever, please, mention the good news in a meaningful way and please, pray that God will enlighten whomever you give to. Christmas could be someone's day of salvation. Jesus came that we might have life, and have it more abundantly (Jn 10:10b).

The real celebration will be later, when we see Him face to face.

There was no room for Joseph and Mary in the Inn. That however did not stop Mary from going into labor. She had her firstborn, a Son, wrapped Him in cloths and placed Him in a manger. (Lk 2:7-8)

Jesus does not force His way into peoples' lives. If they have no room for Him now; He will have no room for them later when He returns. What a tragedy that will be! There are people who actually think God cannot send anyone to hell because He is so kind. They forget, or are ignorant of the fact that He is also just, and His justice demands that sin be atoned for or be punished.

Each Christmas, let's each find at least one person we can share the good news of Christ with. After all, we are God's fellow workers. (1 Cor 3:9a)

Sharing the gospel will accomplish the purpose for which He was born; their coming to faith will be cause for celebration in heaven, in the presence of the angels of God (Lk 15:10).

THE MOST IMPORTANT BIRTHDAY

Birthday celebrations will never be a thing of the past as long as there are people on this planet. Adults and children alike look forward to birthday celebrations each year, either because it is their own or a loved one's. The day is celebrated with a spread of food, drinks, and gift giving. The most unique thing about birthday celebrations is the fact that usually, those who participate in the celebration know the person being celebrated as family or friend, at home, school, work, or as belonging to a special group.

Around this time each year, many people feverishly prepare for Christmas; the celebration of the birth of the Savior Jesus Christ. There are at least three different categories of people in the mad rush. The first group is made up of people who truly know Jesus in a personal way. They have known Him through a personal encounter, they can each say passionately that He is the Son of God, their savior, risen Lord, and coming again King. This group celebrates meaningfully, and rejoices as a demonstration of gratitude for the gift of the Savior.

The next category of celebrants/celebrators knows Jesus by way of head knowledge. They may or may not be church attendees. They know Him as a historical figure, born on Christmas, but they have no personal encounter with Him. They cannot attest to anything meaningful He's done for them. They participate in the festivities anyway, by giving and receiving, being at gatherings and parties etc.

The people in the last group do not have any personal encounter with Jesus; they have no affiliation with Churches, and they may not even know who is being celebrated, let alone why. As far as they are concerned, it's the year-end celebration. They celebrate the same way like the others, with food, drinks, and gift giving and receiving. When it is over, they are glad the stress is behind them. They look forward to doing things differently the next year, either by being a bit more elaborate or spending a little less, or starting preparations (shopping) a little earlier.

Whether people know who is being celebrated or not, it is note-worthy that Jesus is being celebrated. Like the apostle Paul said, "The important thing is that in every way, whether from false motives or true, Christ is preached" (In this case, celebrated). Php 1:18b Jesus' birthday is the most celebrated, more than anybody else's we can think of, from the past or present. The whole world gets excited. The celebration can be a point of reference when we share the gospel with people, just as Paul seized the opportunity to preach the gospel to the people of Athens. He said to them, "Men of Athens! I see that in every way you are very religious. For as I walked around and looked carefully at your objects of worship, I even found an altar with this inscription: 'TO AN UNKNOWN GOD.' Now what you worship as something unknown I am going to proclaim to you." Acts 17:22b-23. So we can introduce Jesus to those who celebrate 'who they know not', by explaining the reason for the season, and why His coming into the world is such a big deal.

SAFE PASTURE IN THE NEW YEAR

The first day of January is always the start of a new year. As many of them as we have seen, we still have no idea what the year will bring when it rolls around. At the beginning of each year, we can look forward with anticipation or with fear of what might or might not be. The only assurance we have is, God is in control and at the right time He will come to rapture the Church. All other issues in our world have uncertainty attached to them. For example, is the recession over or not? Is your job secured? After exercise, good nutrition etc. are you guaranteed good health? The answer to these questions and many others is, "Who knows?"

The Word of God teaches us how to live life until He comes. He says, "Trust in the Lord and do good; dwell in the land and enjoy safe pasture." Ps 37:3

Can we enjoy safety in a chaotic world? Where in this chaotic world can we find this safety? In the land, the Church! That's where! That's where we have the word of God expounded to us. We find support and comfort from each other based on the word of God. "Let us consider how we may spur one another on toward love and good deeds." Heb 10:24

I'm sure there are other pastures outside the church, but they cannot be described as safe. In the world's pasture, individuals are climbing on top of each other and back-stabbing each other to get ahead. Nobody is protecting anyone. There is no shepherd and no under-shepherd. The sheep is destroyed both from within and without.

The Psalmist says in Ps 23:2a, "He makes me lie down in green pastures." As we see, the Shepherd doesn't provide just pastures, but 'green pastures,' luscious pastures to ensure good nourishment.

What the world provides is not nourishment, but rather stress, pain, discouragement, fear, etc. and in the end, death.

Shepherds don't take the pasture to the sheep, but rather the sheep to the pasture, therefore, "Let us not give up meeting together, as some are in the habit of doing, but let us encourage one another-and all the more as you see the day approaching." Heb 10:25

We need to be with other believers as much as possible, so even when Church is officially not in session we can have informal meetings. When we get together, regardless of time and place it is still Church because the Church is 'US' the body of Christ, the bride of Christ. Amen!

Our safe pasture therefore is with each other with Christ as our Shepherd. May the Lord help us to make every effort to remain with the fold, encouraging and being encouraged. Let's be faithful in praying for one another, for prayer is one of the safety gears in the family of God (pasture). Eph 6:18

MEMORIZE: "Encourage one another **daily**, as long as it is called 'today', so that none of you may be hardened by sin's deceitfulness." Heb 3:13

GOOD FRIDAY

Christ's suffering was not accidental, neither was it a surprise; rather, it **was:**

PLANNED—"Therefore, when Christ came into the world, He said: Sacrifice and offering you did not desire, but a body you prepared for me; with burnt offerings and sin offerings you were not pleased. Then I said, 'here I am-it is written about me in the scroll-I have come to do your will, O God.'" Heb 10:5-7

FORETOLD—"He was despised and rejected by men, a man of sorrows, and familiar with suffering. Like one from whom men hide their faces He was despised, and we esteemed Him not. Surely He took up our infirmities and carried our sorrows, yet we considered Him stricken by God, smitten by Him, and afflicted. But He was pierced for our transgressions, He was crushed for our iniquities; the punishment that brought us peace was upon Him, and by His wounds we are healed." Isaiah 53:3-5

"I tell you the truth, one of you is going to betray me." Jn 13: 21b

FULFILLED—"At the sixth hour darkness came over the whole land until the ninth hour. And at the ninth hour Jesus cried out in a loud voice, Eloi, Eloi, lama sabachthni? . . . With a loud cry, Jesus breathed His last." Mk 15:33, 37

PURPOSE—" . . . we have been made holy through the sacrifice of the body of Jesus Christ once and for all." Heb 10:10

"Because by one sacrifice, He has made perfect forever those who are being made holy." Heb 10:14

"This is the covenant . . . I will put my laws in their hearts . . . . their sins and lawless acts I will remember no more." Heb 10:16-17

"And He died for all, that those who live should no longer live for themselves but for Him who died for them and was raised again." 2 Cor 5:15

WILLINGLY AND OBIDIENTLY—"The reason my Father loves me is that I lay down my life-only to take it up again. No one takes it from me, but I lay it down of my own accord. I have authority to lay it down and authority to take it up again. This command I received from my Father." Jn 10:17-18

I am the good shepherd . . . . and I lay down my life for the sheep." Jn 10:14-15

1. ". . . the world must learn that I love the Father and **that I do exactly** what my Father has commanded me." Jn 14:31

OUT OF LOVE—Greater love has no one than this, that he lay down his life for his friends." Jn 15:13

". . . live a life of love just as **Christ loved us** and gave Himself up for us as a fragrant offering and sacrifice to God." Eph 5:2

WHAT SHOULD OUR RESPONSE BE TO SUCH A SACRIFICE?

GRATITUDE: through service.—consider Mary Magdalene. Lk 7:37-38, Jn 20:11

"For I was hungry . . . whatever you did for one of the least . . . you did for me." Mt 25:34-40

LOVE: through worship and obedience "O worship the Lord in the beauty of holiness." Ps 29:2 ". . . Fear him all the earth." Ps 99:5

"This is love for God; to obey His commands." 1 Jn 5:3

TELL OTHERS:—"Go ye therefore and teach all nations . . . . teaching them to observe all things whatsoever I have commanded you . . ." Mt 28:19-20

LOVE AND OBEDIENCE—THE REASONS HE DIED

A popular Easter greeting is, "The Lord is risen! He's risen indeed!"

The first Easter came after a very dark day, a day when Christ suffered at the hands of sinful men. They reviled Him, spit on Him, beat Him, Made fun of Him, made Him carry a heavy cross and then crucified Him. The duration of that agony must have felt like a life time, but after the suffering, Easter came. He rose from the dead. The grave could not hold Him any longer; the tomb was empty and the devil defeated. It was indeed a very mournful day for the devil and his demons. His plans had been thwarted. He had been trying to foil the plan of salvation since the birth of Christ, but his doom was sealed on that first Easter. Amen!

Why did Jesus die? Why did He put up with everything He went through? When the going got tough, why didn't He give up and abort the mission? He could have asked His Father for legions of angels to fight on His behalf, but didn't: and He sure could have called down fire from heaven to destroy those murderers, but He didn't. Why?

He died to fulfill the Scriptures. He died to save us, to open for us the way into the Holy of Holies. Now the gulf between God and man has been bridged by Christ authorizing us to "approach the throne of grace with confidence, so that we may receive mercy and find grace to help us in our time of need." Heb 4:16

Christ has made us acceptable to the Father.

He died out of love for mankind and out of obedience to the Father. In the garden He prayed, "Father, if you are willing, take this cup from me; yet not my will, but yours be done." Lk 22:42

During that bogus trial, when Jesus wouldn't answer Pilate, Pilate said to Him, "Don't you realize I have power either to free you or to crucify you?" Jn 19:10b

Jesus responded, "You would have no power over me if it were not given to you from above." Jn 19:11

Jesus' response proves that man did not have the final word about His death; He could have avoided dying if He wanted to. So what kept Him on the cross? It wasn't the will of man; it wasn't the nails, but love. In John 10 He says, "The reason my Father loves me is that I lay down my life—only to take it up again. **No one takes it from me,** but I lay it down of my own accord. I have authority to lay it down and authority to take it up again." V17-18

Jesus also likened Himself to a shepherd, and as a good shepherd, He laid down His life for the sheep. Jn 10:11

He died so that we won't have to. "I tell you the truth; whoever hears my voice and believes Him who sent me has eternal life and will not be condemned; he has crossed over from death to life." Jn 5:24

He is alive so we can live forever. "Because I live, you also shall live." Jn 14:19b

WHEN GRAVITY BOWS

The law of gravity makes sure whatever goes up comes back down.
Nothing remains suspended, mid-air by itself
But gravity failed when Jesus ascended into heaven
Proving God is the author of gravity and everything else
One of these days, very soon, gravity will fail again
That will be when we are caught up with the Lord in the air

Gravity brings down whatever goes up
But a day is coming, no one knows when
It could be morning, noon, or night
The Lord will descend with a shout,
He will descend with the voice of the archangel
And being the author of gravity, He will again defy gravity

Gravity brings down whatever goes up
But the day is coming when gravity will fail
It will fail when the dead in Christ rise
When the living in Christ are caught up in the air
We will be together with Christ
Nothing can bring us back to earth, nothing, not even gravity

So gravity, where will your power be?
When Jesus, the King of kings appears in the sky?
When His children are caught up with Him in the air?
At the name of Jesus, every knee, including gravity shall bow
Paying homage and worshiping the risen Lord
So shall we ever be with the Lord!

INDEPENDENCE

It has been over 200 years since America declared independence from the British. The implication of that was America was free to do as she saw fit, and it did not have to answer to England in anyway, about anything. America was free to govern herself.

As we celebrate America's independence, year after year, let us reflect on our freedom as Christians. Whereas America's freedom meant independence, the Christian's freedom means dependence upon God through Christ Jesus. We have the freedom to love, to worship, and to obey God.

Cost of Freedom

Our freedom came at a great expense, the death of Christ. "So if the Son sets you free, you will be free indeed." Jn 8:36.

We've been freed from the bondage of sin. ". . . through Christ Jesus the law of the Spirit of life set me free from the law of sin and death." Rom 8:2 "Now the Lord is the Spirit, and where the Spirit of the Lord is, there is freedom." 2 Cor 3:17.

Responsibilities of Freedom

America became free to do as she pleased, but are we free to do as we please? God forbid! Instead, we are free to live in obedience to the one who set us free. "You were bought at a price. Therefore honor God with your body." 1 Cor 6:20 Obedience to Him enables us to live healthy, peaceful, productive lives. "I have come that they may have life, and have it to the full." Jn 10:10b

God's Intention for our Freedom

God is not a slave master, He does not watch over us with a whip in hand, ready to strike at the least sign of failure or disobedience. His plans, intentions, and instructions are not to boost His ego or enslave us; they are for our good. God loves us, He wants us to do well, succeed according to His plan. "This is what the Lord says—your Redeemer, the Holy One of Israel; 'I am the Lord your God, who teaches you what is best for you, who directs you in the way you should go. If only you had paid attention to my commands, your peace would have been like a river, your righteousness like the waves of the sea. Your descendants would have been like the sand, your children like its numberless grains;" Isa 48:17-19a

Evidence of our Freedom (our testimony)

Love for God "Simon son of John, do you truly love me, Feed my lambs, . . . Take care of my sheep." Jn 21:15-17

Worship "Then those who were in the boat worshiped Him, 'Truly you are the Son of God.'" Mt 14:33

Works "For we are God's workmanship, created in Christ Jesus to **do good works**, which God prepared in advance for us to do." Eph 2:10. "Command them to **do good**, to be rich in **good deeds**, and to be generous and willing to share." 1 Tim 6:18. "Our people must learn to devote themselves to **doing what is good**." Titus 3:14. ". . . those who have trusted in God may be careful to devote themselves to **doing what is good**." Titus 3:8

Obedience "If you hold to my teaching, you are really my disciples." Jn 8:31

Love the brethren "A new command I give you; Love one another . . . . **by this all men will know** that you are my disciples, if you love one another." Jn 13:35

Love for neighbor "Love does no harm to its neighbor. Therefore love is the fulfillment of the law." Rom 13:10

FREEDOM IS COSTLY

Every year, we take time to honor our military, both fallen and living. What a tremendous work they do. They protect our country at all costs, both abroad and at home. They leave family and loved ones behind to take on the task of protecting the liberties we all enjoy; liberties like freedom of speech, freedom of religion and the ability to be whatever one wants to be. Sadly, some of these soldiers never return and some never get to see their children born while they were away; they pay the price for freedom with their very lives.

We need to express gratitude more often than once a year for the freedom we enjoy. Due to the freedom they have secured, we are able to gather freely whenever and wherever to worship God without fear of intimidation or persecution from government and unbelievers. Christians in other countries don't have this kind of luxury. They are persecuted constantly and tortured for their faith. As we enjoy our freedom, let's remember to pray for Christians in hostile environments that they will continue to stand firm, that they will be strengthened and encouraged and that through their testimonies their persecutors will come to know the living Savior.

Although we are a free nation, it cost something for us to be free and for us to remain free. There are people who cannot accept the fact that we are free; they are always looking for ways and means to sabotage our freedom. That is why our military is always on the defensive, always ready to fight to ensure that we remain free.

Likewise, Christians have been freed from sin, not by our own doing, but by grace to serve the living God. Our freedom cost God something! It cost Him the blood of His only begotten

Son Jesus. To those who are freed, freedom is free, but to the One who paid the price, it is extremely expensive. Freedom therefore is not free at all.

So what have we been freed to do? We have been freed to live godly lives to the glory of God and to point others in the direction of the cross so they can be freed as well. We have been freed to worship and serve God. We have been freed to serve one another in love, not indulging our sinful nature. (Gal 5:13)

Just as other nations can't stand the freedom we enjoy, the devil cannot stand the Christian's freedom in Christ. He does all he can to re-enslave us from the very things we've been freed from and a whole lot more. Even though we are free we need to fight to stay free; by resisting him through the word and prayer and not yielding when he tempts us. We need to be vigilant because, "Our enemy the devil prowls around like a roaring lion looking for someone to devour." 1 Pet 5:8

Let's keep our armor on 24/7. "Therefore put on the full armor of God, so that when the day of evil comes, you may be able to stand your ground." Eph 6:13a

MEMORIZE: "Live as free men, but do not use your freedom as a cover-up for evil; live as servants of God." 1 Pet 2:16

GOVERNMENTS ARE ESTABLISHED BY GOD

The United States of America elects a new President every four years. For that duration, the President will be the Commander in Chief. Whether you voted for him or not is irrelevant. The Scripture makes it clear, "There is no authority except that which God has established. The authorities that exist have been established by God." Rom 13:1b

If there is no authority except that which God has established, then it is safe to say the elected President is holding that position at that time because God wants it that way. We can choose to follow his leadership or rebel against it. However, since his authority has been established by God, rebelling against his leadership is the same as rebelling against God (except where he clearly violates God's word). "Consequently, he who rebels against the authority is rebelling against what God has instituted, and those who do so will bring judgment on themselves." Rom 13:2

Being elected or established by God does not in any way mean the individual is perfect and will not make mistakes; no human is perfect. It does however mean we should respect him and submit to his authority. Rom 13:1a

Christians have a responsibility towards government. In addition to respect and submission, we need to pray for our government and for those in authority over us.

"I urge, then, first of all, that requests, prayers, intercession and thanksgiving be made for everyone—**for kings and all those in authority**, that we may live peaceful and quiet lives in all godliness and holiness." 1 Tim 2:1-2

Instead of being critical of every little thing that goes wrong, let us channel our energies into prayer that God's will, will prevail in all situations. Disagreeing with something going on in government is not a gauge for God's will. The word of God is! Elijah prayed that there will be no rain for three and a half years; God answered. If we pray faithfully for our government, God will answer.

The elected President appoints his cabinet over the course of a few weeks after his election. It is our responsibility to pray that God will surround him with wise godly men to give him wise counsel. We should also pray that he will be humble enough to listen to his advisers. Finally, we need to pray for his safety and that of his family.

Let's consider 2 Chr 7:14; it reminds us of the conditions under which the Lord will hear our prayers. "If my people, who are called by my name, will humble themselves and pray and seek my face and turn from their wicked ways, then will I hear from heaven and will forgive their sin and will heal their land."